Achilles Alexander Nobile

Miscellaneous Works

Vol.1. Novels, translations, lectures

Achilles Alexander Nobile

Miscellaneous Works
Vol.1. Novels, translations, lectures

ISBN/EAN: 9783337027582

Printed in Europe, USA, Canada, Australia, Japan

Cover: Foto ©Thomas Meinert / pixelio.de

More available books at **www.hansebooks.com**

Miscellaneous Works

OF

SIGNOR A. A. NOBILE.

NOVELS

TRANSLATIONS

LECTURES

SAN FRANCISCO:
R. R. PATTERSON, 429 MONTGOMERY ST.
1894.

L. PERARDI, M. D.
PHYSICIAN AND SURGEON,

Specialita per le malattie di donne.

Office and Residence,
1308 STOCKTON STREET,
Bet. Broadway and Vallejo.

Office Hours
8 to 9 a. m. and 2 to 4 p. m.

UNDERTAKERS ITALIANA
LA PIU' VECCHIA CASA.

IACCHERI & BACIGALUPI
627   BROADWAY   627
☞ TELEFONO 893. ☜

Sola casa italiana che non accetta funerali chinesi. Prezzi modici e massima pulizia. Si eseguiscono e forniscon casse di qualsiasi qualità.

Miscellaneous Works

OF

SIGNOR A. A. NOBILE.

NOVELS

TRANSLATIONS

LECTURES

SAN FRANCISCO:
R. R. PATTERSON, 429 MONTGOMERY ST.
1894.

20177

Entered according to Act of Congress in the year 1894, by
A. ALEXANDER NOBILE, in the office of the Librarian
of Congress, at Washington

A. A. NOBILE.

Achilles Alexander Nobile, the author, and publisher of this book was born in Naples on the 13th day of July 1833. His father was named Alexander Nobile, and the maiden name of his mother was Fortunata Nansò. His father dying of Cholera in the epidemic of the year 1834, his mother intermarried with Frederic Sorvillo.

He received his primary education in the Institute Moccellini at Naples. In 1843 he entered the college of St. Frediano in Lucca, and remained in that institution for eighteen months. He then entered the college of St. Catherine in Pisa. At the conclusion of his course, in this college the University of Pisa conferred on him the degree of Bachelor of Philosophy. This was in 1849. After this he studied law in the said University of Pisa.

At 19 years of age, being spurred on by the ambition common to spirited young men he closed his books, bade good bye to his mother, and started on his travels to see the world.

He traveled around to different parts until the breaking out of the Crimean war. He made a campaign in that under the British flag, along with the Swiss Legion. On the close of that war, he went to South America, and served under the order of Mayor Von Eherenkeutz as Under Lieutenant of Artillery, in the service of the Argentine Republic. Upon the breaking of the war of the Italian Independance in 1859, he returned to Italy, and volunteered as a private in the service of his country. He passed the grades, and was nominated Staff Under-Lieutenant, September 20, 1860. When the Franco-Prussian war broke out, he volunteered again, and served through that war under General Frapolli.

When not soldiering, he was in turn teacher, reader and lecturer.

He arrived in San Francisco in 1889, where he has since remained, captivated by the charms of the city. Here he has learned the printer's art, and established a Weekly Italian newspaper, entitled the "Vespa."

Signor Nobile is also the type setter of this book. Besides this volume now in press, he is engaged on and will publish a memoir of his life and travels which must be very entertaining.

An Anonymous Letter.

I.
THE PUBLIC WRITER.

Fifteen or sixteen years ago, the courtyard of the Holy Chapel presented quite a different aspect from that which it now presents. It is not because many changes have been made, or because the streets leading to it have been improved or widened. No. Everything has remained in nearly its primitive state. The wooden wall which once enclosed the staircase by which the people ascended to the corridor communicating whith the public Hall of the *pas perdus*, though a little elevated, till encircles the old monument; but with the increasing activity which took place in the locality, many of the characteristic marks of old Paris have gradually disappeared. Before the opening of this new thoroughfare the court of the Holy Chapel was almost a suburb of the city where every trace of Parisian society was lost, one after another. This courtyard formed a little world by itself, which had its own invariable customs; now noisy, now silent and always frequented by the same people; early in the morning by the ushers of the Supreme Court who remained till the hour at which the referendaires were used to arrive, by the clerks of a lawyer's office situated upon the treshold of the den of sophistry, and by the housekeepers of the neighborhood, who mingled with the water carriers at the corner of the little street of St. Ann. At twelve o'clock, when all was quiet, the honorable members of public safety, whose barracks were not far off, and who, without any effort of imagination, could have been compared to the *paltoniers* of old times, were used to come to warm themselves in the sunshine. Every day at about the same time the courtyard resounded with the noise of heavy vans whose stables were at the northern corner of the *Corte dei Conti*. At this place, in a recess behind the staircase and precisely under the hall of the first chamber of the Supreme Court had lived for fifteen or twenty years a man called Duverrier, a contractor of the prisoners' conveyance, an industry advantageous enough to allow him the gratification of the luxury of rare flowers, which was his strongest passion. The entrance to the dark cavern which he inhabited, greatly resembled a florist's stall, and the grass which was growing through the pavement prolonged the verdure a few feet further the narrow space which he used as a garden. At twilight, when the monotonous silence was only broken by the steps of the sentinel beneath the gas burning before the palace, this dimly lighted and almost deserted place was the rendezvous of the lovers from the sorrounding streets. Each morning resembled the preceding, always the same events, and, we may say, almost the same conversations exchanged by the same people.

On account of the increasing activity many offices of public writers had been opened around the walls of the Holy Chapel, but at the time when our narrative begins only one of these offices had remained, and it was situated at the right hand of the covered passage leading to the *Rue de la Barilerie.* Every morning the tenant of this hole as big as a sentinel's box used to hang in the most conspicous place a frame containing many specimens of different kinds of writing, which, profusely decorated with flourishes, were hardly intelligible. It was almost impossible for the owner to look at those testimonials of his calligraphic ability without raising his eyes to Heaven, and without heaving a deep sigh, as if they awakened in him the memories of better times, and sorrows at the unjust contempt into which he had fallen.

On the four opaques and dirty panes of glass, through which light penetrated into this box was written in yellow letters: EDITORIALS, MEMORIALS, PETITIONS, LETTERS OF COMPLIMENTS FOR CHRISTMAS AND NEW YEARS," and on the other side: " A. C. TERNISIEN, EX-PROFESSOR OF PENMANSHIP IN THE UNIVERSITY." Notwithstanding the above high qualification and the complete absence of competition, one would infer by the dress of the poor writer that the sign produced very little effect. In winter as in summer his suit was always the same. A black silk scull-cap on which rested continually a hat, made water-proof by a thick coat of grease, while as his only suit he always carried a thin alpaca coat, the original color of which, together with its lining, had ceased to be discernible and whose torn and opened pockets, always empty, yawned at pleasure, a waistcoat with metal buttons, a worn-out pair of black trousers, shrunken and scarcely reaching to his ankles, a very coarse pair of felt stockings and wooden shoes filled with straw, complete the dress; and yet, with all these rags, Ternisien appeared in no way disgusting or repulsive, because in his countenance beamed an honesty and kindness which were not feigned. In him every one could recognize a gentleman fallen from a better condition neither brutalized by misery nor degraded by drunkness, the vice belonging to those who suffer hunger.

His face and hands were always cleaner than his dress; his voice was very melodious; his features expressed resignation, even when, as he daily did, he was complaining to his neigbor Duverrier: and often his complaint would have lasted all day but for the arrival of some customers, who would happen to come and interrupt them.

In spite of his excessive economy, his work would not have been sufficient for his daily wants, if he had not been the possessor of a little capital acquired with great pain in better times, which was destined to buy for him a bed in some hospital, when old age, which was approaching with hurried steps, should deprive him of his sight. For this reason, these savings were sacred to him. He considered them as a deposit which the old professor of penmanship had entrusted to the hands of the public writer. It was very painful to him not to be able to add the interest to the capital. Even if his office had been richly furnished, or in a better location, it is most probable that the upright Ternisien would not have realized profits in proportion to his labors.

The poor man possessed one fault, the drawbacks of which were increased by an exagerated honesty. He suffered from absent-mindedness, and whether he wrote from dictation or he copied, the orthographical mistakes, the repeated words which needed to be erased, multiplied themselves under his pen. Always mistrusting himself and his want of attention, he used to read over accurately what he wrote, making the necessary corrections, and when these were too numerous, he again began his work, without adding a cent to the stipulated price, not wishing to deceive about the quality of his work, nor that customers should pay for his absent-mindedness.

Scruples of this kind in commercial transactions, which ranged from five to twelve cents, made him a real loser each time, as unfortunately for him, his distraction had spoiled a few sheets of ministerial paper.

"Well, sir, what news?" was the question Ternisien used to address his neighbor Duverrier every time he passed his office, while Duverrier never failed to answer:

"May I ask the same of you?"

In this way the conversation, begun with almost always the same preamble, lasted some time. Of course, as every one could easily understand, the first topic was the political situation, which proceeded to the satisfaction of neither. These considerations of high importance being ended, they passed to personal facts. Duverrier, whose business was a prosperous one, avowed himself an optimist, while on the other hand, Ternisien looked at the dark side of everything.

"I am going to give you a piece of good and re-assuring news."

"What is it?"

"Nothing of importance. While I was watering the flowers, Mr. B., the referendaire who is in the good graces of the president, approached me with these words: "Mr. Duverrier, you have very beautiful camelias." For your sake I seized the occasion, and I took the liberty of presenting him with a few Timoleon's bulbs for a garden which he rented at Passy."

"If you have done this in my interest," answered Ternisien, "I thank you very much, although, my good friend, I shall beg of you to explain to me what I have to do and in what way I am connected with this business."

"You must have heard of a scheme to beautify our courtyard of the Holy Chapel. Now guess, if you can, what were the intentions of these gentlemen? Now, since

I found you a protector, I may tell you without fear. Well then, they intend to destroy your office and send you elsewhere to carry on your business."

"Indeed?" exclaimed Ternisien with the expression of a person about to lose what he wrongly called his supporting business.

"Yes," added the other; "but be at ease. As I have told you already, I took advantage to speak of it to Mr. B. He has a certain esteem for me, and you will not remove."

Those last words ought to have brought back to the lips of Ternisien the usual smile, but his thoughts had fled to his situation, and instead of smiling he heaved a deep sigh.

"Are you sorry?" asked Duverrier.

"No, no, on the contrary; again accept my heartfelt thanks. At least hope will be left to me, and hope is something, although alone it cannot enrich us. Listen, my friend, now my profession is not worth a cent. Innovation has killed us. In France nothing is permanent. Every day brings new changes, and old habits are as well loved as cast-off clothing. Arts, which were once praised, are now despised. What good can you expect from such a state of things?"

"Upon my word," answered Duverrier, "I can't understand what you are complaining of. For my part I believe innovations are very excellent indeed. Mankind tends always to perfection, this being one of the laws of society. For example, my father used to convey the prisoners in cars, which brought so many shocks that, at the moment of leaving, the poor men were obliged to review their teeth in order to see whether they had lost any. I, on the contrary, carry my prisoners in carriages, so soft, that they are as comfortable as if they were on the best coach. Do you see anything bad in this improvement? I do not.

"Possibly," said Ternisien, " the same does not happen to me. When first I established myself in this abode I had some little profit. From time to time I chanced to have a good job, which gave me time to wait patiently and which made up for the days I was without work. Near by, at the lawyer's office, I had splendid customers. When they had plenty of work and wished to enjoy themselves, they furtively brought to me copying to do. They paid without bargaining and without a murmur, and the work was easy because they recommended me to do it in the most unintelligible manner."

"And why, please, do they not call any more on your talent?"

" Because they don't need it. Have not lithography and type-writing been invented? The work is done quickly and at less cost. It is thus that artists become ruined. I shudder to think of it; it is the last blow given to penmanship. I, who now am speaking to you, once used to give lessons at sixty cents each; I have taught the position of the body and how to manage the pen to lads of the first families, to misses who had hands whiter and softer than the paper on which they used to write. I taught in a college of the capital, and, to become perfect, two years of application were necessary. We taught by principles, and slowly, while now some charlatans, who have turned everything topsy-turvy, pretend to teach penmanship in six weeks. All that made me shudder. Truly, I am no longer a young man, but my eye is good and my hand does not tremble yet, and if the old methods were esteemed as they deserve, I should not be a public writer.

Ternisien had never before delivered so long a speech. He felt the need of resting himself, wiped his nose and offered Duverrier his snuff-box.

The latter took advantage of this pause to say:

"Why do not employ the new methods if the old ones are no longer useful?"

"I!" replied the old professor with a look of contempt; "I! Should I then have wasted twenty years of my life in studying the art of writing well? Should I have overcome all the difficulties and learned all the forms of penmanship—*round hand*, *Gothic*, *Italian*, etc.—only in order to approve now with my example a bad innovation? Never! And by the way, do you know this renowned and extolled invention, about which Carstairs and his pupils made so much noise? It is simply the inclined calligraphy which they impudently have disfigured and by a mechanical process, apart from intellect, have made uniform for everybody. And here is where the evil lies! A cook may write as well as his own teacher, and their own handwriting will be similar that no difference can be distinguished, and then of what use will be that other useful and precious art of guessing the moral character of an individual by his handwriting, I should ask you. No, no, Chrisostomus Ternisien will never countenance the propagation of such impious inventions. I am ready to change my profession, and by compelling me to leave the place they will perhaps confer a favor on me."

His interlocutor was already preparing himself to ask of him the explanation of these last words, but was prevented from doing so by the arrival of a lad between twelve or thirteen years old, resolute in his bearing, bold and quick like a true *gamin* of Paris, who, turning his eyes from one to another, ended by asking:

"Are you the writer?

Duverrier went away, leaving Ternisien alone with his customer.

"What do you want, young man?

"I wish you to copy this," answered the youth, showing him a piece of paper which he folded in his fingers.

Ternisien glanced at it without reading it, and only assured himself of the quantity of the work. After this first inspection, going out of the shop and bringing his customer before the frame, he asked him:

"What sort of writing do you wish?" and with his fingers pointed out the different specimens.

The lad looked at him, and finally told him to choose the cheapest.

Ternisien went to his seat, prepared a beautiful sheet of paper, cut a new pen and began the reading of the manuscript. After a few lines he stopped, raised his eyes to the little urchin, who was standing with his shoulders against the posters of the door, and, who with crossed arms and legs, was whistling an air with variations of his own. Any one, who might have observed the looks of Ternisien, could have easily perceived an expression of doubt and astonishment, when he turned his face to the boy.

In a moment he opened his mouth as if to call him, but seeing him so careless and so little concerned regarding what passed on behind his shoulders, he pursued his reading. As he progressed, his eyes became animated; curiosity and interest appeared in his face, it seemed that he was trying to solve a problem which required all the force of his imagination.

The boy continued to whistle as a lark, and Ternisien did not mind it.

Having taken the pen, he examined it, putting it between him and the light, and already dipping in the ink and flourishing it, was ready to trace the first letter, when suddenly he entered into a new and different order of ideas. Hesitation succeeded the interest with which he had read those lines. Evidently he struggled between the mechanical work of his profession and the appreciation of the writing he had under his eyes. Ternisien's intelligence was not bright; constantly closed in the narrow circle of a specialty, which did not require any effort of imagination, he confined himself to the form of the thoughts without trying to penetrate them. He was like those materialistic philosophers to whom the creature hides the creator, and inasmuch as misfortune has always the sure effect of reviving conviction in men who are suffering, the more his name was spurned, the more he exaggerated his own importance. Of all his sufferings he had formed a sort of religion of which he was the martyr. But if in his poor brain reason had darkened itself to such an extent, his soul had kept its candor and all its primitive uprightness. Straightforward with his customers, he was also straightforward with himself. His pride as professor was mortified at descending to the position of an employee, and he only yielded to necessity every time that for a moderate price he wrote insignificant lines; but he often shuddered when he thought that he might lend the aid of his pen to sinful words, and feared that he who was incapable of telling a lie even for his own advantage, sometimes might be an instrument of calumny and falsehood. This has been precisely the secret feeling he intended to express when he had said *compelling me to leave this place* they will perhaps confer a favor on me. His impossibility to exercise any other profession obliged him to remain in this. The writing to be copied was of such a nature as to inspire him with reflections very embarassing to his conscience.

In spite of his cleverness in interpreting the handwriting of these lines, he remained uncertain, and convicted of impotence in the same way as an academician stands in the presence of a hieroglyphical inscription. His position was graver and more serious. Of what interest in history indeed is a false statement or mistake? What is falsehood or truth to those who are dead, and even to those who are alive? In his case instead, although he did not know by whom the letter had been written, nor to whom it was addressed, nor what sincere or perfidious interest had dictated it, he was afraid when he thought of the consequences that letter may bring. The wretched man, lost in this labyrint, had vainly asked advice of his usual counsellor. He rolled between the thumb and forefinger of the left hand a pinch of snuff which he took from time to time; he applied to the gift of writing the same apologue Esopus had applied to the speech, and allowing himself to be carried away by the strenght of his learned digressions and by his classical remembrances, in a solemn voice he cried:

"If like Achilles' spear which cured the wound made by itself!"

"What is the matter?" asked the boy, turning around, "have you finished perchance?"

"I have not yet began."

Oh! perhaps you do not know how to write, or are you waiting for some one to help you. Give me back my paper or hasten, I am in a hurry. Somebody is waiting for me."

"Perhaps the same person who gave you this letter?" asked Ternisien.

"No, but some of my friends with whom I was playing marbles. I left my turn to another boy who does not play so well as I, and having ten cents in the game I would be glad to know how business is standing. Quick'y, move around, double quick, as I have yet another errand to do; are you perhaps frightened about the payment? Here it is, I pay you sixteen cents in advance. I do not wrangle, but I am in a hurry and you must be quick."

Without being moved, without sharing in this impatience, the old writer said to the boy:

"Who send you on this errand?"

The boy looking at him, answered:

"Somebody," and then turned up his nose and stuck out his tongue and his lower lip. Any other man would have punished this very disrespectful act, but the kind old man renewed the question.

"If formerly I answered you somebody," said the boy, "it is quite clear that you ought to know no more than that. What else? They gave me the letter with the instructions to have it copied by a public writer; they gave me the money and I went away to execute their orders. I pray you, why then do you not do your duty? That's all. Would you like me to whistle you anothe air? Perhaps it will please you," and he began to whistle a ballad which was then very popular———

"When love was constant, etc."

Ternisien again put before him on the table, which was his desk, the letter and the paper, and again took up the pen. It was not the desire of earning the sixteen cents, magnificent recompense for a few minutes' work, that had decided him to do it. He had made two very easy reflections which overcame all his scruples: firstly that what he was going to write might as well be true as false; secondly, that if he should refuse, a less scrupulous colleague would do it. It must be said that he was much moved by curiosity, and he was waiting for the time when, according to the instruction given (without doubt) to the boy, he would write tha name and address of the person to whom the letter was addressed. Nevertheless, before beginning to write, he asked:

"Have you read this letter?"

"I? I can't read. I do not know the name of the letters and I would be sorry to be a learned man as you are."

"Why so?"

"A nice question! Because you would not have had the pleasure of my acquaintance, and I that of telling you that you would do better to move your pen than your tongue. The person gave me this paper asked me, before all, if I was able to read, and I answered no. Then I received my instructions with three francs, of which I shall give you sixteen cents, if you make haste, and you instead are going slow as a snail."

Ternisien, seeing that he would not obtain any further information, began his work. He had so attentively read and weighed every word of the paper that he had almost learned it by heart. Every word expressed such serious facts, such important revelations, that they had engraved themselves in his memory so as to prevent any possible distraction. Contrary to his habit, he copied the paper without a single mistake. As soon he had done he folded the sheet, and turning to the boy he said;

"Did they give you the name and address to which it is going?"

"Yes" answered he, extending his hand to the table with celerity and without being noticed, " yes it is written with pencil on a piece of paper which is in the left pocket of my waistcoat, but you must not know it."

At the same time, he took the letter and jumping backward moved to leave the shop.

"Some other one is going to scribble this address," he added; "I have my orders."

"Give me back that letter," asked Ternisien; so many precautions do not mean anything good."

"No," answered the boy, I will not give it back, and even you will return to me the copy I have brought you.

or you will tear it in my own presence. **This order has been** strictly given **to me."**

" Even that!" exclaimed the writer, clasping his **hands.** "Ah! from this time I swear never **more** to copy anonymous letters. They surely intend to destroy the traces of this one, and I ought have refused it."

"What a stupid old **man,"** said the boy; "he looks as if he were saying his prayers. Well, then, good man, you must come to a decision. Tear up the paper or you will not get your money." And the sixteen cents from the table had returned to his hands. Searching on the table for the paper, which in the first movement he had pushed away and mixed with others, Ternisien tore it in a thousand pieces and threw them in the face of the boy, saying to him:

"Away with you! young rascal."

"A rascal? Yes, but not a thief," replied the boy; "here is your cash." And taking his aim, he threw the eight two-cent piece into the big pocket which yawned at the side of the writer's coat, and in which they fell as in a ravine. He then retired, walking backward and laughing at the ex-professor, and bold **and impudent,** went away like a sparrow who laughs at those **who try to catch** him.

Ternisien for **a** while remained in deep meditation. At last he got up, put his papers in order, took with him **a sheet** of paper, shut his office, and crossing the courtyard, **went to** speak with his neighbor who was watering **his** camelias.

The boy, faithfully following the orders he had received, brought the letter to another public **writer** and then posted it. It was addressed:

JULIUS VALABERT, Esq.,
Auditor of the State Council,
Rue de Lille, 34.

II.

THE LOVERS.

What we have narrated is in a certain way, the prologue of our tale. We must go back a little to present to our readers the principal persons who will figure in this story. And to begin, we will introduce them to a house in Furstemberg street, in the most distant part of St. Germain's thoroughfare.

The apartment in the second story is neither rich nor luxurious; there one does not see expensive furniture, nor rich curtains, nor costly bric-a-brac,—in the parlor only a looking-glass, in the windows plain cotton curtains, some easy chairs but not a sofa, a bare ceiling and a simple carpet, green like the wall paper of the room. The only object which seemed of any value was a piano of the newest fashion, out near which were piled many books of songs and complete operas. In spite of the modest value of the objects which furnished this principal room, the good taste which had presided over the harmony of the whole gave to it an aspect of elegance, and it could easily be surmised that this so clean and so well-kept apartment belonged to a lady.

In fact, near the window, before a tapestry frame, a beautiful person was seated, hastily finishing a very pretty piece of work. She was dressed in white, and the simplicity of her toilet harmonized thoroughly with that of the place in which she lived. Her long dark eyebrows, lowered upon her work, rose only at intervals, and then her beautiful dark eyes turned to the clock, the hands of which seemed to move too quickly for her. Her hands, of a wonderful whiteness, could have served as a model to a portrait painter if the extremity of the fingers had been thinner. Her neck, finely shaped, was of perfect form and beauty, and imparted grace and flexibility to every movement of the head. Finally the moment arrived when the young girl consulted the clock with pleasure and cut the last thread of the tapestry.

Getting up from the chair and giving a last glance at the whole of her work, she rang. An old servant appeared.

"Marion," she said to her with a joy which sparkled in her eyes and was evident in her voice, " at last this work is finished. What do you think of it?"

Marion approved with majestic air, and struck with the brightness of the colors and exquisite taste with which they were arranged, exclaimed: "It is a masterpiece! if you would let me act according to my own fancy, you would receive a better price."

"You know that every work is already sold at the same store and for the same price."

"Jews!" murmured the old woman.

"It isn't right, Marion, to treat in such a way kind people who have procured for me a steady and sure resource, which supports me."

"Oh! upon my word, if you would, you need not work."

A severe look stopped the words of Marion, who turning her eyes in another direction, replied with great embarrassment:

"I meant to speak of your talent in music; there are few teachers of your ability, and when you used to give lessons at two dollars each———"

"That displeased Julius."

"It is true," answered the old woman, " since then you play music only for him. To tell the truth, I prefer this life to the old way of living, always in town and alone, whatever might be the season, while at present you do not go out any more, except when Julius gives you his arm, which happens very seldom, indeed."

A second look from the mistress ended Marion's babble.

While she spoke, the young lady had taken the tapestry from the frame and folded it with great care.

"Be quick; take it away before Julius arrives," said the young woman, "and hide the frame so that he cannot see it. This is his hour."

"Be careful; Master Julius does not like mistery."

"Alas! God only knows how much it costs me to have a secret from him.

She made a sign and Marion went out, leaving her mistress in deep thought, this brief conversation having been sufficient to recall to her mind her present situation.

Fanny was three years old when she lost her mother. Her father, a teacher in a provincial town, spared neither pains nor trouble to educate her. His dear and only daughter was always the first and best among his pupils. Showing a decided inclination for music, a competent teacher was given her. In everything she progressed rapidly, and in a short time her father was able to see her as perfect as he wished to be. She was scarcely sixteen years old, when Mr. Dusmenil, satisfied of having warned her in general terms against the dangers which threaten a maiden, gave her a freedom which, for a heart naturally tender and open to impressions would be dangerous. Among other liberties, he permitted her to remain long days togheter with a neighbor's son named Ernest, a young man rather good-looking, who lacked not cleverness. It is true that Mr. Dusmenil saw in Ernest, educated with his daughter and until that time an innocent companion in her studies and plays, the future husband whom he secretly destined for Fanny, and, therefore, did not discourage an intimacy which would afford them the opportunity of mutually knowing each other. This time that which had been anticipated did not happen.

Fanny, in the presence of her childhood's friend, experienced no emotion, either because her hour had not yet arrived or else because it is almost impossible that true friendship should change in love.

The time was passing pleasantly and her future seemed smiling and flattering, when she was overtaken by a dreadful misfortune. Her father died almost suddenly, leaving no fortune. Ernest was then absent, and his family, on account of Fanny's poverty, did not show further desire to carry out the proposed marriage.

Fanny resolved not to wait for Ernest's return and left, retiring to an old relative's whose only assistance consisted in advising her to employ the little money she yet possessed in developing her talents and in taking a few lessons before begin to teach. She soon succeeded in securing a few pupils, by which means, little by little, she derived a certain amount of comfort.

One day she was called at a house in the *Ghaussee d'Antin*, to teach music to a young lady about ten years old, named Eliza Saint-Gilles.

The family into which she was introduced consisted of influential people, proud of their riches. Being requested to play, she performed a selection which enraptured all these present. Among others, a young man made himself conspicuous for his lively admiration, although Fanny, on her part, paid no attention to his compliments. The following day, at the time of the lesson, the young gentleman happened to be in the room and continued to come every day, sometimes at the beginning and at other times at the end of it. His eyes constantly fixed on the teacher, forced her to blush and in spite of herself troubled her. Chance, one day, left him alone with Fanny at the moment in which her lesson had ended and while her pupil was going out for a walk. Persuaded that he would find little severity in a young girl who was living alone and who, on account of her profession, was dependent upon the public, he spoke to her of love with an air of assurance and self-conceit, and tried to approach her.

A gesture full of dignity forced him to stop.

"I am an orphan," she said to him; "I have no relative, no defender; my only support is this," pointing to the piano, "and you are trying to deprive me of it, because it is certain that I should no longer dare to come to this house."

After saying these words, Fanny went out, but on reaching home, still affected and her eyes filled with tears, she received a letter in which Mr. Julius Valabert, acknowledging what kind of woman he had offended, presented his most respectful apologies and entreated her not to add to the faults with which he already reproached himself that of having caused her departure from the house of Saint-Gilles, and promised her never more to go there. If Fanny had a mother, her conduct would have been different.

The culprit's repentance found favor with Fanny. The fear of an unpleasant scandal if the reason of her not going any more to the lesson should have been suspected and the security inspired by this letter, caused her to return to Mrs. Saint-Gilles' house. The young man appeared no more. The human heart is always full of strange contradictions, and even the sincerest is the most ingenious in deceiving itself. Fanny on returning on that house, had really thought she would not again meet Mr. Valabert; and yet, without knowing it, she was dominated by a vague hope that Julius would come in person to present his apologies. Vainly she prolonged her lessons beyond the time she ought to have given them; the interest which she used to take in the progress of her pupil was no longer the same, and her zeal in teaching was infinitely diminished.

Was she comprehending her real feelings? No; without doubt she did not understand herself until the day when, arriving earlier than usual, she noticed the presence of Julius.

By the blushes which she felt suffuse her face, by the sudden palpitation of her heart, she understood what she had tried to hide from herself, that she loved Julius.

When he timidly asked of her, as a great favor, permission to be present at the lesson, she had no strength to refuse him, so great was the inward joy. That day she accompanied badly and sung out of tune, but on the following day, already prepared for the presence of Julius, who did not move from the parlor, she sung with such expression and threw so much soul into the notes that the enamored and ecstasied youth could only thank her with his eyes for the pleasure he had felt in listening to her. The girl's joy was intense and noticeable. A few day afterwards they ventured to sing together, a dangerous experiment which was repeated many times, and the harmonious, fascinating music achieved the seduction.

This would have been the right time for her to fly, but she had not the courage to do so. No one was there to teach her that sentiment of reason which she lacked, and not knowing how to close her ears against the language of a young and sincere lover, she had the weakness to betray herself.

On his part, he passionately begged of her to grant him the happiness of seeing her alone and of being received at her home; his grief was so violent, his tears so sincere, his passion so prevailing, that one day he knelt at the feet of Fanny, in her little apartment in Furstemburg street. Alas! Poor Fanny had no mother to watch on her.

Six months after, when we meet Fanny, in spite of the great love of Julius, which seemed to increase daily in intensity, she felt a deep and strong sorrow which poisoned her happiness. At the side of Julius she endeavored to overcome it, asking from love the oblivion of her remorse. But in the hours of solitude and reflection, a lively grief mastered her heart, tears flowed abundantly as soon as her thoughts departed from the present, marching toward the future. Her only hope reposed on the uncertain duration of the love of Julius. For although he was most tender and affectionate, yet he had some faults which rightly grieved her. The principal ones were mistrust and jealousy. Already to please him, she had decided to discontinue her lessons, as Julius thought her profession a little precarious, because he, with his experience, had learned to what dangers a young teacher is exposed; and although renouncing in this way the exercise of her talents she had lost much, yet she would accept nothing from her lover. Fanny succeeded in persuading Julius that she had still a small income arising from the united legacies of her father and an old aunt which, together with savings, (now almost exhausted,) was enough for her needs. We have already seen how the poor girl added to her scanty income by the sale of her tapestry-work, in which, as in many other things, she was indeed very skillful.

Very few minutes had passed since Marion had gone, when Fanny was disturbed in her meditations by a sharp pull of the bell, which restored her gayety.

"At last!" she thought, and run to open the door.

Julius entered. He was a young man about thirty years old, with dark hair and rather pallid complexion. The habit of serious study had imparted to his countenance a premature gravity, and although naturally kind and inclined to indulgence, one might have noticed in his looks that distrust common to all those who on account of their studies, keep aloof from the world, and who are not accustomed to judge of men and things at a single glance. At the moment Julius appeared, he had the thoughtful mien of a man who has taken an important resolution and had prepared himself to disclose it. After having glanced around him, he asked where Marion was.

"I sent her on an errand," answered Fanny, without any further explanation.

Julius entered the parlor, took Fanny's beautiful hands in his own, kissed them, and mentioning her a seat, seated himself near her.

"Fanny," he began with the sweetest voice, "Fanny, are you happy?"

"Certainly," she answered, "how could it be otherwise? Is not your love always the same? Every time you wish to know if I am happy, ask yourself if you love me."

"Yet, nevertheless," replied Julius, "you are suffering without confiding it to me, as if your heart were hiding something from me. More than once I have discovered traces of tears in your face; more than once I thought I had guessed the agitations of your soul. From whence that grief which your feigned gayety cannot hide from me? Speak, Fanny, have confidence on me; what do you wish? What do you require of me?"

"Nothing! Have I not told often you that your love is enough for me?"

"Do you not possess it entirely? I know well you do not ask for splendor, or luxury, or the pleasure of vanity. You refused my gifts, and I was obliged to yield to a pride I so much appreciated. Fanny, that which you wish for, the desire which troubles your joy and quiet and perhaps injures your health also, is then greater than my riches, greater than my love?"

"Can you think so?

He smiled sweetly, adding in a most encouraging tone "Speak, tell me it, open your heart to me."

Fanny answered: "Friend, I do not complain of my own lot, I made it what it is. I love you, and so long as you will love me I shall have no other grief. Forgive me if some remembrance of the past comes to my mind, and tries to disturb the happiness I feel with you. Alas! despite of myself, against my wishes, sometimes, I often fancy to see my father, my poor father who loved me so much, appear before me with angry face, asking a strict account of the principles in which he had educated me, I have no reason to reproach you. I asked only for your love, and until now you have given it. You had only promised me faithfulness, and you have kept your promise. What reason have I, then, to complain? What are the causes of my grief? I am happy, you know it very well."

While saying these words, she wiped a falling tear.

Julius pressing her head to his breast, answered:

"Yes, dear Fanny, without doubt I promised you my love, but this love is capable of anything; it will not stop short of sacrifices which will cease to be called such the moment when through them you recover your peace and happiness.

"What do you mean?" she asked, raising her beautiful eyes, full of wonder.

"Yesterday you confided me something."

She blushed and bent her head.

"To day I answer with another confidence. My family wish me to marry."

"What then?"

"Well I have resolved to choose a companion, but I will not go to find her among the women belonging to the class of those apparently wealthy but poor in true merit, in whom vanity corrupts the best sentiments—among those ladies who think that a great name or a great fortune can dispense with virtue or talent. No; she whom I choose will be a timid and modest woman, whose heart I have already learned to know, sufficiently in love to have yielded to me, sufficiently virtuous to feel repentant—a woman, in short, who is worthy to bear the name of an honest man. You, Fanny, are that woman; that name is mine. I offer it to you; do you accept it?

The poor girl listened as if she could not understand his words. When Julius had finished, she remained a little while with her hands clasped and as though she were yet listening to him.

Julius took her hand and gazed at her lovingly.

"Is it true?" she said at last; "is it not a dream?"

"No, no; it would be too cruel were it not in earnest."

"Oh! dear!" and while so saying she let herself fall into his arms, but soon freeing herself from him, she fell upon her knees, exclaiming:

"Oh! my father!"

A thought crossed her mind, and raising, she approached Julius, and regarding him fixedly all the time she was speaking, said:

"Thanks, dear, for your generosity. If you could read my heart, what gratitude and new love would you discover in it. I have yet a question to ask you. Listen: these words are serious, and I pray you seriously to answer them. If what you told me is only dictated by conscience, if you offer me your hand, this precious present by me so long wished for, only as a performance of a sacred duty, if some day, in the future, your heart should murmur against the sacrifice you are making for my sake, then how great will be my grief; and although I have no right to think of myself alone, yet I should prefer to hide my loneliness and shame in some unknown place rather than to live with you, spurned and despised by a husband who would soon repent of the concessions given in a moment when passion overpowered him."

"Fanny," replied the youth, "I swear to you that my heart only has urged me to take such a step."

Again she fell at his feet. He raised her, and in a few minutes Julius was kneeling before her, saying:

"Now, Fanny, will you refuse me what I am going to ask of you."

"What can I refuse? What do you wish of me?"

"A proof of love. As you well know, I always feared that your heart, before being acquainted with me, had loved another. You have always assured me of the contrary, nevertheless this fear often returns to my thoughts. To day I doubt no more. I can assure you of it. You have told me a thousand times that you have kept nothing of the past but remembrances of your childhood and of your family. You have jealously kept as a treasure a ring, in which your mother had put a lock of your hair when you were so young you could only answer her by caresses. I wish to have this ring; give it to me—to me your lawful husband, now that in me is concentrated your whole family that you have lost. Give me what remains to you that belonged to your mother.

She was about to rise, but pausing, "Later," she said.

"Why not now?"

"Dear, I always believed in the sincerity of your love. I inferred it from your jealous fears, and my only sorrow was in not being able to quiet your suspicions. All you have now told me certainly fills me with joy, but does not at all surprise me. I was waiting that word which should take away all guilty from us; I was waiting because I knew you loved me, also because you are good and generous. Listen, then: On the day of our marriage I will give you that ring, which I cannot part from except for the sake of him whom I love. This has always been my thought. On the happy day of our union I cannot put on my head the orange crown every bride is accustomed to wear in going to the altar. That ring is the only thing I have not given you. It will be my nuptial gift."

Julius would, perhaps, have insisted, but just at that moment Marion entered. She seemed disappointed. By means of signs, she made her mistress understand that she had not found the usual buyer and that consequently she had brought the tapestry back.

"What is the matter?" asked Julius, who had already noticed some of these signs.

"Nothing," answered Fanny, smiling.

"Always some mysteries!"

"No" and she embraced him.

In order to change the course of Julius' thoughts, she added:

"Have you pondered over all the obstacles to this our happy union?

Before he had time to answer, a loud noise was heard in the street, usually so quiet. Julius ran to the window, and a few steps from the house he saw a fainting woman sorrounded by a crowd. He immediately descended into the street in order to bring help, and a few minutes afterward he returned.

"Strange," he said, "the horse of my cousin, Mrs. De Launay, who had gone to her business man to take an important document, has fallen, and although not wounded, the fright has experienced has caused her to swoon.

I shall go and see her home. Good-bye, darling, till to-morrow————"

Embracing Fanny, he quickly departed. Fanny went to the window to see him go. Julius dare not to look at her.

III.

THE FRIEND.

On the following day, while Julius was at Fannys' house, a scene was enacted in the street of Lille, the consequences of which might have destroyed all the projects of the two lovers. Mrs. Valabert had received a visit from the Countess of Septeuil, a lady of ancient nobility, immensely wealthy and in friendly intercourse with many persons having influence at court.

The conversation between these two had been quite long. As this visit was a very important and not an ordinary one, the conversation, at the beginning cold and reserved, had gradually become lively and confidential, till both ladies, after a long diplomatical discourse, had thought it convenient to explain the cause which had brought them together.

The interview had ended, and Mrs. Valabert was already accompanying the Countess to the door of the hall, and the two ladies had reciprocally exchanged parting salutations, friendly, although full of dignity, when the arrival of two other persons delayed their separation a few minutes.

One of the two comers was a gentleman of about forty or forty-five years of age, with an open face which indicated most splendid health and complete absence of all sorrow. His manners were those of a man who, although accustomed to mingle in high society, lacks grace and elegance of carriage. His prominent gray eyes expressed a constant satisfaction and happiness. He held his head aloft like those who, proud of themselves, believe that they produce in others the same favorable impression they feel whenever they place themselves before a mirror. Mr. Saint-Gilles had left the army at the time of the second restauration and thrown himself into speculations, and, like many others, had succeeded without knowing what he was doing. Chance had made him a wealthy man and riches made him fat. The person who accompanied him was a young lady who may have been about twenty-six years of age, and who appeared neither more nor less. Her features had kept the freshness and delicacy of youth, her smile was enchanting and all her movements were calm, pleasant and symmetrical. Her beauty was not that which strikes one at the first glance, but rather that which insinuates itself little by little and engraves itself on the heart, and which, though scarcely exciting desire, is yet the most certain to retain the love it has produced. Her dark complexion was in strong contrast with her blue eyes and fair hair, but these almost sure signs of a passionate organization, in which are mixed two different and opposite natures, voluptuous languor and ardent vivacity, were belied by her quiet behavior and an expression of kindness. When she used to raise her eyes toward any person, one would say that she was looking for some grief to console, and would suppose that only the troubles of other people could ruffle the quietness of her soul.

In spite of all these qualities, Adele De Launay had never been happy. At twenty-one she had married a man twice her age. Not having known love's infatuation, she had not even had the opportunity of experiencing that quiet happiness which surely possesses a greater value and lasts longer. Her husband was one of those men without virtues or vices, whose lives run from one project to another, planning schemes which are soon given up for new ones; one of those incomplete natures without will or patience, that vegetate everywhere without bearing fruit. She had followed him to various cities where he had gone for foolish experiments or for industrial speculations, and the clearest and most evident result of all these journayings had always been the same, a loss of time and capital. Finally, after many years of this roving existence, Mr. De Launay, almost ruined but not reformed, had been enticed in a new scheme which had allured him on account of his remoteness and the probability of its success. With the remains of his fortune, he had laden a ship with goods which he intended to sell in South America at fifty per cent. profit, and this time he had put himself at the head of the expedition, having agreed with his wife that she should remain in Paris while waiting for the *galeons*.

Of her own dowry Mrs. De Launay had saved one hundred thousand francs, which her husband could not touch. Mrs. Valabert, her distant cousin, who had many times good occasion to appreciate her, had requested her to come and reside with her. Adele had accepted this offer, which, at the same time leaving her free and mistress of her movements, afforded her protection and a home befitting her age and position, and she had now being residing in that house for six months.

Saint-Gilles, on perceiving the Countess of Septeuil, assumed a more contented air, and his eyes were enabled to express something a little resembling thought. With an awkward and very evident intention of joking, he addressed a few complimentt to the noble lady, and congratulations upon meeting her at Mrs. Valabert's. On her part, Adele De Launay had contented herself with boving to Mrs. Septeuil. As soon as the Countess had left, Saint-Gilles and the two ladies went into the parlor There Mrs Valabert addressed Adele thus:

"Cousin, you well know our agreement, absolute and full freedom as well for you as for me. This morning you wished Saint-Gilles to accompany you while shopping at several places. Be pleased now to give him back to me as we have need to converse together."

"Since you wish to be alone, I will retire."

"Before you go," replied Mrs. Valabert, "allow me to repair an involuntary negligence. Yesterday I was somewhat ill, this morning you went out early without my having the pleasure of seeing you. I hope that you have not received bad news?"

"None, my dear cousin," answered Adele, "and I thank you for the interest you take in all that concerns my welfare."

After these remarks, she retired to her own apartments.

Saint Gilles gazed after her, saying:

"That crazy fellow, De Launay, is happier than he deserves to be. Here is a woman who loves him in spite of all his extravagancies. If he would write her to join him, I would not be surprised if she should at once obey. While he could have quietly enjoyed such a treasure at home, he become a merchant of Cologne water and English soap in the other hemisphere. There are some persons, who although their heads were full of eyes, would not be able to see clearly."

"Yes," answered Mrs. Valabert, sadly, "there are passions impossible to be explained; some spurn virtue, some do not know vice."

"Oh!" said Saint-Gilles, who had already without ceremony seated himself in an easy-chair, his legs crossed and his body reclining, "what has happened? Did the Countess departed disappointed?"

"Yes; friend."

"Why so."

"Because there exists an obstacle which you do not know, and which we cannot say that we will be able to overcome."

"What is it?"

"It is just to speak to you of it, and to ask your advice that I have wished to be alone with you."

Mrs. Valabert brought another easy-chair near Mr. Saint-Gilles, and sat down beside him.

Before we let them begin their confidences, it is necessary to explain briefly the friendship which existed between these two persons.

Saint-Gilles was a bachelor. Mrs. Valabert was a widow, but (which is rarely the case) their relations were truly based upon pure and holy friendship. Julius' mother was virtuous not only on account of her training but by nature. Cold and calm in her youth, she had never admitted the possibility of a fault, and the love which enraptured the senses, love without marriage, was considered by her a chimera or a vice without excuse, like hypocrisy, falsehood or theft.

Saint-Gilles had received many favors from Mrs. Valabert, for which he had shown himself very grateful. He continued to visit the widow, and little by little made himself indispensable to her. He had no equal in bestowing trifling attentions and in busying himself with other people's affairs. Always at the disposal of whoever needed him, he collected rents, canvassed for mortgages to place money, arranged preliminaries of marriages and took upon himself all sorts of troubles and every kind of work. In short, he was a most clever and indefatigable "*factotum.*"

"Friend," began Mrs. Valabert, "to you I am indebted for the acquaintance of the Countess of Septeuil. You were the first who thought of this marriage, so advantageous for my son. The Countess gave her consent to this union, and has given me the assurance that her daughter made no opposition to it whatever. With sorrow I have discovered a secret which for a long time I had suspected, namely, that Julius had a guilty connection with a person whom he is passionately in love with."

"Oh!" replied Saint-Gilles in a very easy way, "at his age that is a very common occurrence."

"Yes, but he will not part with this woman."

"Poh! Julius is a young man of spirit, who will not sacrifice his future to a caprice. Be at ease. Besides he knows of the negotiations begun with the Countess and he has already seen her daughter. It is true that he has not consented openly, but neither has he refused. If he had not had good intentions, he would not have allowed us to take these steps, since at the point we have now arrived, it would be almost impossible to break them off without a strong and reasonable motive."

"We have not positively consulted him, and have only taken his silence for consent. Perhaps Julius does not even know that the Countess came this morning to visit me. Do not be mistaken about the character of my son. I can and do know it better than you. He is a man who waits for the last moment, not only to make a definite decision, but also to communicate to you his resolve. To display courage, he needs to feel danger. He loves me, it is true, but although his love is sincere and deep, he will not yield to me."

"And who is the object of his passion?" asked Saint-Gilles, "perhaps some common woman? perhaps an actress? perhaps a dancer?"

"Whoever she may be, she must be a woman of loose habits," replied Mrs. Valabert, "as I have been told she is young and beautiful; she belongs to an honest family, and unhappily it seems that she has received a splendid education. She is a piano teacher, by name, Fanny———"

"Fanny Dusmenil?"

"Exactly that. Do you know her?"

"Certainly. For some time she gave lessons to my little niece. Beautiful creature! a beautiful morsel, I swear to you. What eyes! What beautiful hands! and to all that she adds talent, great talent indeed! Julius saw her at my sister's house. One day she sent a message notifying us that she could not come any more. No one could guess the reason of such a resolve, but now it is all explained. Upon my word, nobody would have surmised it. With her modest demeanor, she must be an old fox. She must not be allowed to go umpunished. Where does she reside?"

"Near here, in Furstemberg street, I believe."

"I will run there at once," said Saint-Gilles raising."

"Dear friend, I never doubt your interest in me and in all that concerns me. Before taking any steps, I must ask another favor. Instead of going to see this young girl, who would surely complain of it to Julius, exaggerating your words, would not it be better to address your remarks to my son? I hesitate to speak to him. He is no more a boy; I cannot scold him, and in spite of my love, I could with great difficulty decide to be a witness to his blindness and to hear him praise the woman who deceives him, for how we can believe in the virtue of a woman who even for once has forgotten her duty?"

"It was my intention," answered Saint-Gilles, "to employ the quickest means to cut the evil at its root; but, as you wish it, I will speak to Julius. It is impossible that he will not recollect himself. Did they tell you that he intended to marry her?"

"No, but if perchance he were about to do so?"

"Oh! before all," replied Saint-Gilles, "we must not trust this princess. I pretend to be a good physiognomist, and yet I would have given her the communion without confession. We have no time to lose; all these creatures have a fondness for marriage. I hope Julius will open his eyes. He is in love. Very well; he will fall in love with his bride, who is also a beautiful woman, and after eight days he will think of the other no more. After all, we have a last resource to dry the tears of his Ariadne. What does she wish for? A position? money? we will give her half of what she asks, showing ourselves good and setting the matter conveniently. With twenty to twenty-five bills of a thousand each, all will be made right. With this sum we shall send this young lady to her penates and her music with variations, and after a time she will marry some young artist, whom she will make happy. I will take it into my hands and then who shall know? Though I am not severe like you, I think it really very probable and possible that she may deceive Julius. I can easily believe that a woman, if mistress of herself can very well avoid lovers, but as soon I know she has a lover, I am justified in supposing her with two lovers. We shall see; and while we are awaiting the result, try to cheer yourself."

The conversation was pursued a little further, and Saint-Gilles persuaded Mrs. Valabert not to alarm herself for the time being, and to continue the negotiations with the Countess. His arguments with Julius did not secure the result desired. The reader will excuse us for not repeating here the very excellent reasons he presented and urged in speaking to Julius; it will be enough for him to know that none of them were received with favor. Saint-Gilles belonged to that class of persons who believe in being useful to others by giving them advice for which they have not asked.

The happy tranquillity of that family was completely changed. Julius, fearing his mother's tears and prayers, avoided her presence as much as possible, and, when with her, kept a cold silence. Vainly Adele De Launay endeavored to enliven the conversation. She showed herself more than usually good, thoughtful and amiable, but no explanation had ever taken place in her presence; neither had she been admitted into confidence, so that, granted that she did not know the cause of this coldness, she was in no way authorized to provoke a decisive explanation. Julius, on the other hand, had completely concealed from Fanny the opposition he experienced from his mother, whose mouth-piece was Saint-Gilles. He strengthened himself in the resistance, always fearing the moment when in a irrevocable manner he would be obliged to signify his firm resolve. He hoped that Saint-Gilles, acknowledging the inutility of his attempt and tired of the struggle, would cease his annoyance.

In this false situation many days passed, but the catastrophe was destined to come. One morning Mrs. Valabert's house took on the appearance of festivity; the servants were going and coming with a busy air. Julius, on returning home at noon, noticed all this stir, and was at a loss to know how to account for it. Just as he was going to ask the reason of it, the door of the parlor in which he was, opened. Mrs. Valabert was coming from her apartments, dressed and in the act of going out.

Stopping before her son, she said to him:

"I am very glad to meet you. I hope that you will have no engagement for this afternoon, and if you had intended to go out, I beg you to sacrifice this evening to me, as I am expecting a numerous company."

"Whom?"

"Many friends among whom will be the Countess of

Septeuil and her daughter."—"Madam!"——interrupted Julius.

But his mother, who had spoken these words almost hurriedly, as one who could see no reason for objection, had already crossed the parlor. A servant came to tell her that the carriage was ready.

In his first emotion of surprise, Julius had let her go. Immediately he understood that, by disposing of him in such a way, his affectionate mother had made the last effort. Thus he would have been under the necessity of letting others believe in his silent approval, or by refusing to be present to break all the negotiations, which could be considered bad manners, and would have compromised even his mother. And yet this was the only course left to him.

This elaborate snare, so easily to be avoided, in which they were trying to entrap him, was more unbearable than serious and strong obstacles. He had seated himself, pondering how to act. Julius thought himself alone, and was amazed to feel a hand laid on the back of his easy chair, while a sweet voice thus spoke:

"You are sad, cousin; is it not true?"

Julius turned and saw Mrs. De Launay gazing at him with interest.

"How long have you been there?" he asked. "I do not remember have seen you come in."

"I was in your mother's room. I arrived just when she left the drawing-room, but lovers have neither ears nor eyes, and I am not offended at your absentmindedness. All your attention must be given to HER."

"Then you know all?"

"Yes; this evening party had already been arranged four days ago. It is a little plot prepared by Mr. Saint-Gilles, to which my cousin has given her consent. Neither the former nor the latter will believe that your love is deep and sincere."

"And you believe it to be so?"

"If I ought to have been a diviner, as neither you nor your mother ever spoke to me of it. All that I do know I have learned from your sadness and from some few words heard by chance or willingly listen to."

"If they had consulted you, what would have been your answer?"

"I should have refused to enter this plot."

"Why?"

"Because one cannot betray one's allies."

"Then you pity me?"

"If I had not, would you see me here?"

"Kind Adele, I am suffering; yes, I am unhappy."

"And, nevertheless, you love and are loved?"

"Without a shadow of doubt."

"What else do you want? A happiness which only depends upon yourself! Listen to me: I always thought that women, better than men, know how to love, because when they feel a strong passion, they do not look at the difficulties and are ready to defy death, while you men do not know how to bear a moment of embarrassment or of shame."

"You are right; I am feeble, and I fear to bring affliction on my mother."

"Or, perhaps, to repent yourself some day?"

"Oh! never, never!———if you know her!"

"Speak to me, then, with open heart. I fear that all that I am now to do or to say may be wrong. I ought to remain neutral. But a friend will be allowed to ask for your confidence, when another has taken upon himself the right of torturing you without consulting you. Answer me, then. Is she beautiful?"

"Without her I cannot live."

"She is beautiful, yes, without doubt, but I meant to

say remarkably beautiful———"

"More so than yourself, my cousin;" but he soon added, "at least I believe so"

"Are you sure of it? and do you not deceive me? Has she spirit?"

"Very much indeed and, joined with simplicity, that spirit which comes from the heart, like yours, cousin."

"Pray do not use me as a comparison," answered Adele smiling, "and I am not questioning you to hear her praises. After all, you love her, and this is the main point. Are you sure that she also loves you, and that she never loved another? Is she virtuous?"

"He who would try to say the contrary must prove his word or I should have his life."

"Oh friend! if your heart would be completely free and you would be the absolute master in choosing a wife could you dare to hope to have in her united, talents spirit, virtue? and because you have been so fortunate as to find such a woman and to possess such a treasure, you spurn it! And what for? Julius search your heart. Have you never reproached her with the love you have inspired in her?"

"Can you judge me so unjust? No; Fanny, in my eyes, is the most virtuous woman in all the world."

"Marry her, then, and do not ask me for advice."

"I shall take advice only by myself, my good cousin. My present embarassment lies in finding a way to break this projected marriage."

"It is your own fault. Why have you not spoken a month ago?

"I am well decided not to appear this evening, but how shall I avoid a scandal?"

"I do not see any way. The rupture ought to come from the Countess, not from you. Were I you, I would not worry myself until to-night. Yes, on my word. Who knows but some good angel will watch over you? Often, just when we feel very unhappy, we find ourselves near to happiness. Hope! these moments of tranquillity will be so many stolen from future grief, and perhaps even these last will not come."

Before Julius, who shared not this confidence, could ask her what cause inspired her with it, the drawing-room door opened and Mrs. Valabert came in. She had a serious and preoccupied mien, and was crumpling in her hand a letter which had arrived in her absence and which had been given her by the porter on her return.

"My son," she said, in a voice which hardly concealed her emotion, "you are free and master of your evening. Lady Septeuil writes me that she is not able to accept my invitation. Send a servant to Mr. Saint-Gilles, and, if he is at home, tell him to call as soon as possible," and she departed, murmuring a few words that her son was not able to understand.

This second apparition, so different from the first, amazed Julius. Glancing at his cousin, he said:

"Adele, what were you saying a little while ago; that the rupture ought to come from Mrs. de Septeuil? But this seems a true rupture; you, perhaps, were cognizant of it?"

"I had hoped for it."

"The angel who was watching over me was then you?"

"Hush!" said she, "be silent!"

He replied in a low voice: "But how it happened all this? Please explain yoursef, that I may be able to thank you."

"What I have done is of little importance. I will tell you about it later, if you will be so good as not to reproach me with having guessed what you had not told me. Now let us part—not a word more, not a sign nor a look of intelligence. I saw you so unhappy, here is the excuse and explanation of my conduct; to morrow, or in a few days, you will entreat your mother, and she, perhaps, will be moved by your prayer. Do not vaste your time with me, go to HER; go, friend, and love her always because she is worthy of you. Good bye."

Mrs. Valabert's pride had been offended by the action of the Countess; and the latter was too proud to retract. All the diplomacy of Mr. Saint-Gilles failed to bring about a renewal of the negotiations. Mrs. De Launay fearing sooner or later she might be involved in these family discussions, went into the country for a few days, to the residence of a friend of Julius' mother.

Julius was not able immediately to obtain the consent he asked for. Every time Mrs. Valabert was moved by her son's prayers, Saint-Gilles, who had considered as his own business the rupture of this marriage, reproached her with her feebleness. Saint-Gilles had not been able to put in execution his first scheme of addressing himself to Fanny, because Julius was continually with her. Finally frightened at the anxiety and agitation of her son, Mrs. Valabert yielded on condition that she should not see her daughter-in-law. Julius at about twenty leagues from Paris, owned a villa which was comprised in his father's estate. The interesting condition of Fanny not permitting him to present her in society, he had resolved to take her to this little country residence. In order to announce her the day fixed for the marriage and make known to her his last arrangements, he went, as usual, to the house in Furstemberg street.

Occupied with his thoughts, he was walking rapidly Just as he was nearing the door of Fanny's house, he encountered upon a young man issuing from it. While ringing the bell, his heart was trobbing. He reproached himself for the injurious suspicions continually torturing him in spite of his love. On entering, it seemed to him that Marion was confused and that Fanny blushed when he narrated his encounter, but he ended by being ashamed of his jealous suspicions, and soon restored by Fanny's tender and affectionate looks, he forgot all to think only of the near future which promised to be so calm and happy. The villa to which he intended to take his wife had not been inhabited for three years. It was necessary to put it in order. It was agreed that Julius should go alone and remain absent from Paris for eight days, the time to complete the preparations.

From the moment when they had begun to love each other, this was their first separation, and although it would last no long, the parting was as painful as if they were never to meet again.

On his return to Paris, Julius Valabert received the anonymous letter copied by Ternisien, the address of which, as stated in the first chapter, had been written by a different person.

IV.

THE TRIAL.

Seated in the same room where we saw her before, Fanny let her eyes sadly wander from the window to the door, listening to every noise and showing in her features fear rather than hope. Do you remember with what joy she had been animated when Julius brought her the announcement of his resolve? Why, instead, we do find her so sad to-day? Because the nearer the time appointed for her nuptials approached, the more she felt her heart oppressed by a fatal presentiment. Eight days had already passed since Julius' departure, and this absence, the first she experienced, had left her alone with the fears of her heart without defense, and at the same time exposed her to some intrigues which had poisoned her solitude.

The day following the departure of Julius, a gentleman whom she remembered to have seen previously at the house of her young pupil, Miss Saint-Gilles, had called on her and without preamble or formality had spoken to her of the schemes of Julius' family, of the brilliant hopes destroyed by his love for her, of the grief that every one had felt and the pain with which they had consented to this union, and finally he mentioned a last hope founded on Fanny's generosity, that she might persuade Julius himself to consent to what was wished from him. Saint-Gilles did not forget to adorn his speech with flattering words and praises: Fanny would be esteemed by everybody; no one would be surprised to hear that she herself learning of the existing difficulties, had sacrificed her own love to the future happiness of Julius; that all knew her to be so unselfish as not to hesitate before such a sacrifice. They knew also that she was so sincere in her love that she would prefer the interests of Julius to her own. All these things had been spoken cautiously but with a tune in which one could easily perceive the skepticim of a wordly man, ready to deny every kind of true and sublime affection. There still remained the last alternative, that of **pecuniary** compensation in exchange for so many destroyed hopes. Although Saint-Gilles had relied very much upon the strenght of this argument, he dare not speak of it. Fanny's demeanor had made such an impression on him as to prevent him from uttering the words, "*pecuniary compensation.*" Saint-Gilles took his leave without receiving a positive answer, but obtained from her a promise to let him know her decision.

The following day, after a night of wakefulness and fever, she sent him a note containing these simple words: "*Address yourself to Julius.*" Thus the negotiations were sent again to the same field on which he had always been beaten. These attempts, this appeal to her generosity and this exaggerated picture of Mrs. Valabert's grief destroyed Fanny's confidence by showing the present full of struggles and dangers, the future dark and uncertain For the first time she paused to ponder on the intrigues and plots of every kind which a powerful and also ambitious family might organize against her. She had been unable to give a very clear answer to Mr. Saint-Gilles, because she dare not to reveal to this railer the sacred motive which made it a duty for her to resist his insinuations.

"If instead of this man, " she said to herself, "Julius' mother, with eyes full of tears, had come in person to me, I would have thrown myself to her feet and spoken thus: ' Pity, and do not despise me. If it were only a question of my happines, I would sacrifice it without hesitation, if I had only to renounce Julius, although I love him with all the strenght of my soul, I would depart, I would hide myself, and neither you, nor he, nor any living person would hear of me again. Perhaps finally he would be able to forget me and might some day be happy, and you enjoying his happiness, would think of me absent, and in your heart thank me, and this thought will bring consolation. But, alas! if I should act in such a manner; another voice would rise to accuse me, a being dear to me whom I must love as you, madam, love your son, would ask of me an account of a sacrifice which would deprive him of a name, of a family, of a future, and you, yourself, who are so good, would you advise me to become a bad mother?' "

Carried away by her grief for an instant, she thought of going to Mrs. Valabert, to declare all to her and place herself under her protection, but was prevented by shame. If she had been acquainted with Mrs. De Launay, that friend so sincere and indulgent, whose generous act Julius had narrated to her, she would have confided in her and thought herself safe. Timidity detained her.

Thus for eight mortal days, alone, a prey to her fears, she saw no other help than Julius, who was absent, and whose weakness of character she dreaded. How many varied tortures afflicted her mind, always disposed to exaggerate evil! The humiliation she expected and the repentance that Julius would perhaps experience when his passion had abated, would leave him under the ascendancy of his mother. Perhaps, also, that jealousy which he was unable to control, would, some day, bring him to suspect her who had not known how to resist his seductions because, strange as it is, ladies are always punished for their sins by the same persons for whose sake they sin, and who gather in the fruit of their crime

In this manner, after the infatuation of her passion, Fanny was experiencing the first trial of life, and, instead of peace and happiness in her soul, she met doubts and fears at every step.

As a last refuge, there remained to her the remembrance and thought of Julius. She plunged so deep into it as to forget everything else. Had she been possessed of cooler blood, or, better, had she a more complete knowledge of evil and of the advantage that slander takes of every circumstances even the most trivial, she would have anticipated by her explanation the unhappy circumstances which might cloud her reputation. She would have felt the necessity of giving an account and explaining another mysterious visit she had received after that of Saint-Gilles. Her love made her forget all this, her only thoughts being of her Julius.

At last, as we have said, the eight days of Julius' absence were past. She was waiting for him, when she was aroused by a sharp pull at the door-bell.

"Here he comes!" she cried and ran to the door.

Julius entered.

Fanny's joy was of short duration; Julius seemed not the same man. His face was fearful pale, his eyes glaring, his lips trembling. She tried to speak, but courage failed, and in silence she stood gazing at him. Without uttering a single word, he shut the door and hurriedly crossed the room. Fanny followed him.

Julius cast at her a dreadful glance, which seemed to penetrate her heart. One of his hands, placed under his coat, was agitated by a convulsive movement. With the other he seized Fanny by the arm, forcing her to remain at his side.

"What ails you? Julius you frighten me."

"Sit down" he answered with a gloomy and threatening voice.

She sat down mechanically, subdued by that command and the gesture by which it was accompanied.

Julius had made an unspeakable effort to overcome the emotion which oppressed him. He was no longer able to restrain himself. For a few moments he was silent, as if collecting himself to enjoy at his leisure the continually increasing agitation of the unfortunate Fanny Then, without even ceasing to stare at her, as if he wished to test her, he coldly and briefly said:

"So then you have deceived me?"

The poor girl, dumb with amazement, threw herself back. In her turn she felt the words dying on her lips, and her voice strangled in her throat.

Julius, who yet held her by the hand, and who saw her cast down by such unexpected accusation, shook her fiercely, and with a tune full of rage, continued: "Answer, answer me!"

Vainly he endeavored to awaken her out of that dreadful dream. She answered no more, inasmuch as the thought of being adjudged guilty had never occurred to her mind. All her preceding fears were justified; the intrigues, the plots she dreaded came to attack her. Fearful suspicion! Julius, perhaps loved her no more; Julius, conquered by the prayers of his family and in compact with them was now searching for a pretest for a rupture. A fearful abyss had opened at her feet, and she had fallen into it. Julius afraid of such an easy triumph, repressing himself, thus continued:

"I shall try to be calm. Listen to me. This interview, perhaps, will be the last one between us; if you cannot justify yourself, it will be an everlasting rupture, but I shall not judge without having first heard you. If you have deceived me, you were very guilty, because I had perfect confidence in you; I would have been ashamed of watching your conduct. I loved you and to you I would have sacrificed all,—friends, fortune, mother—"

Fanny made a movement. Finally she understood that she was accused of infamy and baseness. Blushes suffused her face and her cheeks, and when Julius asked her for an answer, she, this time purposely remained silent because she felt wounded in her virtue.

Another pause followed, and Julius began:

"Speak to me frankly, Fanny. Am I the only person who has put the feet in this apartment?———Think well. Have you received any other?

" Ah! if that is the question," she replied, "yes; another person has been here whom you know, one of your friends, Mr. Saint-Gilles."

" Saint-Gilles!" said Julius, completely astonished.

" By his remarks he prepared me for this altercation."

" He? He must explain to me his way of acting. It is not of him that I am speaking; you do not speak to me of another man whose mysterious call has been revealed to me."

" Ah!" answered Fanny, "what has been reported to you?"

"This is what I have heard," cried Julius, rumpling a paper which he took from his breast: It has been narrated to me that during my absence, the day before yesterday, in the evening, a young man wrapped in a cloak had entered your house, secretly introduced by Marion; that he had left two hours after; that this young gentleman had called often, though you had never spoken to me of it; lastly that he had known you before me, that he loved you, and that you were to marry him. Is all this true? It is necessary that I should tell you his name?"

"It is needless," replied Fanny with dignity: "who gave you these particulars?"

"This letter," said Julius, "can you contradict it?"

"Who signed it?"

"Signed it is not, but what care I if it tells the truth?"

"An anonymous letter!" said she with contempt; and you trust it? A vily denunciation has in your heart a stronger influence than the thousand proofs of love which I gave you? You have for me so much esteem that the first comer can slander and calumniate me without being forced to answer for his saying? Ah! sir, what future are you preparing for both of us?"

"Instead of accusing, defend yourself. If the author of this letter has stated a falsehood, I will discover him, and I swear by heaven I will punish him. But if, instead, he has opened my eyes in regard to you and to a perfidy of which I would have been the victim, then he is a friend and it is my duty to thank him. Hear what he writes, and afterward tell me which name he deserves."

Opening the paper, with a chocking voice he read:

"*Sir*:—A person who takes an interest in you, but who
" wishes not to expose himself to the hatred of any one,
" thinks it his duty to take the veil of the anonymous to
" enligthen you about a woman who is on the point of
" receiving your name. I do not know whether you
" were the first in her affection, but I do know that you are
" not the first that ought to have led her to the altar. A young man of her own place, united to her by a friendship of long standing, was deeply in love with her and he
" ought to marry her. This union cannot be compared
" with the one you offer her. She had to renounce him, but
" in doing so she has not ceased to see him. At the
" beginning of your acquaintance, he presented himself
" at her house. Afterward he called again; once you met

"him before the door, and now that he is obliged to
"depart, she has received his farewell. Your absence
"from Paris favored this last meeting. Yesterday evening,
"Mr. Ernest Gairal, with many precautions, entered her
"house, and after two hours he left."

"Forever," exclaimed Fanny, rising, "forever!"

"You then confess that he has come?"

"Yes, please now listen to me."

"No, nothing! nothing!" replied Julius, **raging**.

"Listen. One condemns a person, then, without allowing her to answer? I am innocent. I was wrong in keeping it a secret because of your jealousy, which I feared. This young man had been choosen for my husband by my father. For him I did not experience either hatred or love. I left my birthplace without even telling him. He came here once to remind me of the intentions of our respective families, and I did not give him any hope, although I did not then know you. He loved me, it is true; that he returned to visit me is also true; and the day before yesterday he again returned. I did not conceal from him my love for you, or your generous conduct, nor the destiny which awaits me. He left me resigned, and, as I told you, forever. For me, dear, this visit had no importance; it came unexpectedly, and if I have not spoken to you before, it is only because it passed away from my mind."

This defence, so simple, had destroyed, little by little, almost all the suspicions of Julius. In proportion as she spoke, the confusion and agitation of his heart faded away to give place to the shame of having shown himself so cruel. Moved by the sincere tone of these explanations, he was already prepared to fall at the feet of that woman who had once more become his idol, when his eyes rested on the end of the letter, which he had not yet read. He wished for a final trial.

"Forgive me, Fanny. I ask you a thousand pardons if I have wronged you or suspected you unjustly. My excessive love made me unjust. Be not provoked at my anger. The secrets hidden by you may serve as an excuse for this moment of rage. Do you forgive me?"

She placed one of her hands on her heart, and offering the other, which he covered with kisses, said:

"Ah! Julius, what pain you have given me! I should never have thought I could suffer so much without dying."

"Now," he added; "as a guarantee of this reconciliation, give me the token which till now you have refused—the ring, the only souvenir of your mother. The more dear it is to your heart the more acceptable to me will the sacrifice be."

Fanny answered, smiling: "Have you forgotten what I have already told you? Why this so earnest desire? And what high value could it have to you?"

"Does it not contain the hair of my Fanny—hair taken from her head when a child? Do not refuse it to me, I entreat you. I know where you keep it. It is in a little casket at the bottom of the first drawer of this *secretaire*. Please give me the key."

His looks were always sweet and affectionate, but his voice trembled and had a strange tone of rage. Fanny perceived it.

"Oh!" she said, "you are asking for your pardon."

She hid the key in her bosom and withdrew a few steps.

"I do wish it," cried Julius, giving free course to the anger he had restrained with so much difficulty. "I do wish this key, I need it, even if I must wring it from you."

"Always suspicions."

"Always some mystery!"

"Well, then, I shall disclose you everything. If till now I have refused to you to open my *secretaire*, it was only because in it you would find some accounts, some documents which would have revealed to you that instead of living upon an income bequeated to me, as I always told you, I lived by my labor. I did not confess the truth to you, because I was too proud to accept your gifts. Have I committed a crime? and those who have written to you will they yet maintain that I am a woman moved by interest?"

"Then you could deceive me for so long a time, and you could repeat to me this falsehood so many times without my dectecting it, so great was the sincerity which shone in your face, so innocent was your mouth, as it is at this very moment, in which you are again deceiving me." So saying, he wrong the key from her hands.

Amazed by such violence, Fanny fell senseless into the arm-chair. Julius opened the *secretaire*, then the drawer and the casket—but the ring was not there.

"Ah!" he exclaimed, "I was quite sure of it."

At these words, Fanny recovered her consciousness, ran to the *secretaire* and also began to search.

" My ring! my ring!"

" Disappeared!"

" Stolen!"

" Yes, stolen," repeated Julius, and violently seizing the girl by the arm, he thrust the letter before her eyes and finished reading it aloud:

"'The proof, sir, that all the relations between that
" woman and her first love are not ended, the proof that
" they loved each other and that Gairal's departure had
" for its purpose only to facilitate an advantageous marr-
" iage, is in the fact that before they parted, she wished
" him to accept a family ring which had belonged to her
" mother, which she jealously kept, and in which was
" enclosed her hair."

" Well pursued Julius, " Will you deny it now? This ring you had refused me; the key, too, you were refusing not long ago. Knavery on knavery! Falsehood on falsehood! Treachery on treachery!

" Marion, " cried Fanny.

" Ah, you well know that she is not at home. I alone will answer you. I curse you and hate the day in which I was acquainted with you. Farewell! farewell! Say to your lover that he can return. "

In departing, he cast a last look at Fanny. She was lying on the floor immovable, pale in a state near to death He made a few steps to help her, but his feelings of anger and contempt returning, he called an old woman, her neighbor, and after pointing out to her the fainted Fanny:

" Take care of that woman!" he said, and, throwing her a purse filled with gold, disappeared.

V.

THE AUTOGRAPH.

At the moment in which Romeo receives from the servant, Balthazar, the news of Juliet's death, he pronounces these simple words: "Indeed! Now, enemies stars, I challenge you!" and afterwards buys the poison. This deep grief, so parcimonious of complaint, impresses more than any exciting paraphrase. In fact, our nature usually takes interest in the doings of our fellows, whatever they aim at, and sometimes even when their sentiments and feelings are not in harmony with ours. This interest lasts while hope supports it and uncertainty delays the result, but from the moment in which his destiny is accomplished, it is necessary that he in whom we were interested spare us his joy or grief. A settled matter excites our attention no longer. We, too, will spare our readers the description of Julius Valabert's mental sufferings.

After the dreadful scene we have narrated, we will pass over an interval of eighteen months, and we shall find him one year married, and at the moment in which the wife opening the door of his office, with a sweet and timid voice says to him:

"Excuse me if I am intruding, but the person you send for has arrived. Do you wish to receive him now, or do you prefer he should wait."

Julius had married his kind cousin Adele De Launay Very few words are necessary to explain the change which had taken place in the respective position of these two persons.

As a result of the rupture with Fanny, a violent fever

had endangered the life of Julius. He would certainly have died without the constant care of his mother and Adele. Friendship and love had restored him to life. A deep sadness and protracted languor followed his delirium; without opposition he allowed himself to be carried to the country, where, according to the doctor's opinion, the pure, fresh air would restore his energy, and where the sight of new objects would cancel, little by little the remembrance of the sad event. In company with his mother and cousin, he went to the neighborhood of Lyons. There was a moment when they thought to have the company of Saint-Gilles, but the presence of this gentleman was obnoxious to Julius, who did not doubt that the anonymous letter was his work, although inwardly he sincerely thanked him for having enlightened him. All that reminded him of the infamous treachery, caused painful and grievous emotion. Perhaps in his heart, he had flattered himself with the expectation of receiving a letter from Fanny, in which she should try to justify herself. However, he had not heard from her; all those who approached him kept silent, and Julius, blushing and ashamed of his weakness, dare not to confide in any one of his friends.

Thus he left Paris hiding in himself the dumb grief which gnawed within, too offended to think of a reconciliation and to deeply in love to unbosom his grief to others.

But every hour which passes pours a drop of balm into the most painful wound, and every day which dies takes away one of the thorns which make the heart bleed. During the first few months passed in the country, Julius felt no sensible improvement. The days were excessively hot and the sultry nights were too oppressive for his feeble constitution. The flowers, which were in all their beauty, their perfumes, the golden fruits of the earth, the plains covered with verdure, the thick foliage of the woods, that powerful germ of life which abundantly circulated in nature, all these beauties of the sky and the earth, oppressed him as a stinging irony, as a complete contrast with the desolation and the dryness of his soul, in which nothing grew except a bitter agony which he persisted in keeping hidden. However, little by little, flowers withered, autumn appeared with its train of shadows and air filled with dew, with its pale sun shining through fogs as a smile through tears. Julius felt his intense grief partially dispelled. The sadness and mourning of the objects which sorrounded him harmonized with his own sadness and invited him to confidences.

His solitary walks were replaced by others with his mother and Adele De Launay, and between the latter and himself a greater intimacy began. The woman who had once foreseen his desires, who had shared his hopes, ought she not naturally to be the first to console him? Only with her he dared to speak of Fanny. In these long private conversations, which became of daily occurrence, in those prolonged communings by the fire in the evenings, she narrated by what means she had caused the rupture of his marriage with Miss de Septeuil; how without any one knowing it, an act justified by her intention, she had in her hand the thread of that intrigue; how by means of suspicions dexterously insinuated she had prepared the Countess for the first refusal; how, at the same time, having learned that Miss Septeuil, with no love for Julius, only obeyed her mother, taking advantage of that first moment of spite, she had advised a prior suitor to renew his courtship. From confidence to confidence she ended by revealing to him a secret that she had concealed from all in order not to add her own griefs to those which Julius already suffered. She had not wished to take for herself any of the consolations due to him. Mr. De Launay had died, and that sad intelligence had been received by Adele a little before the time when Julius had thought he was betrayed in his love. Julius was never tired of admiring such inexhaustible kindness, always ready to sacrifice for others. This treasure at this moment belonged to no one. Their interviews becoming longer and more frequent, and without having lost any of their intimacy and pleasure, were sometimes timid and embarassing, both for him and for her. Fanny's name was no longer so frequently spoken, and, one evening Julius holding his cousin's hands and fixing on her glances which troubled her, asked her if she would finish the work begun, and reconcile him completely to life, granting the happiness he had never known.

" We have both suffered," said he. " Married to a man who was not able to appreciate you, you had patience and resignation: I, on the contrary, experienced violent and strong passions. To day, both free,—you from an imposed chain, I from my error,—we feel the need of a quiet and sincere affection. Be mine, if not from love at least from pity, and I will be grateful to you for it. "

Without answer on her part two months later Adele had married her cousin.

The year following their marriage was spent in the country. Mrs. Valabert's death strengthened these ties.

At the beginning of the winter, they returned to Paris. Julius resumed his occupation, for a long time interrupted, and searched for relief from those sorrows of which the stings had not yet disappeared, in work rather than in the pleasures of luxury and of the world. Saint-Gilles, during this long absence of Julius, had resumed his old habits. He rarely called on him, and obedient to Adele's prayers, had always avoided speaking of the doleful past.

To the work which had usually kept Valabert busy, had been added others, viz: the putting in order of family papers, the examination of the titles of succession, the copying of letters and other papers. He had, therefore, given orders to search for an honest and reliable man to whom could be entrusted a little work, and as we have said at the beginning of this chapter, his wife had announced to him the arrival of that man.

To the question, " Do you wish to **receive** him? " Valabert had answered with an affirmative nod.

" Dear, " added his wife, " would you permit me to remain present? "

" Without doubt; but what inspire you with this desire? It is only a question of figures and documents, and in all probability the conversation will be very wearisome. "

" I spoke for a moment to the person introduced to you, and, if I do not mistake, he is an original full of many pleasant fancies. "

" Wery well; judge him for yourself. Let him come in. "

An old man presented himself, and **his** entrance justified the words of Mrs. Valabert. Arrived on the threshold of the room, he saluted them in an awkward way and with an exaggerated politeness. With both hands he removed an old hat, the edges of which were broken, and by a hasty movement of his head in bending it to the knees, he had caused to descend over his forehead the torn edge of a dirty silken skull-cap. As if this ridiculeous salutation were not enough, he repeated it three **times** at intervals, each time advancing two steps, without perceiving that Mrs. Valabert and her husband were making useless efforts to restrain their laughter. As soon as the poor man had ended his genuflexions, he raised himself up, **casting around** timid and humble glances.

Suddenly his face assumed an expression of astonishment, and he stood before Valabert with open mouth and distended eyes. Adele watched this inexplicable pantomime, when her husband, his thoughts returning to by-gone times, exclaimed:

"Ternisien!"

"Mr. Valabert!" answered the ex-professor. "How! you have had the kindness to remember my face? Have yet not entirely forgotten him who taught you the principles of an art which is now spurned, and of which perhaps I am the last representative? The times were very different when I used to come to give you lessons in St. Honoré street, where your father lived. It is now eighteen years since I saw you last, and I remember you always because you were kind and affectionate to your professor. I beg pardon, madam, for thus speaking in your presence, instead of waiting the permission of your husband, but thinking of that time, I seem to become younger. Look here, madam, you must not pay attention to my dress. This morning, in order to come to you, I have brushed and darned these rags as best as I could, but they, I know very well, are old and in bad shape. On entering I felt ashamed, and if you had not been present, I am almost sure your servants would have thrown me out like a beggar. Then I become confused and made very humble salutations that I might be forgiven my presence and intrusion into these rich, splendid apartments. Once I, too, knew how to present myself properly, madam, and I have punished many young ladies, rich and beautiful like yourself."

Adele smiled kindly, which finally put Ternisien at his easy.

"Truly," replied Julius, "I am happy and glad to meet you again.

"And I, too," answered Ternisien. "Well I can see you are not changed; always good and without pride. As you take away all my embarrassment, I shall ask permission to sit near the fire while you explain how I may serve you. It is long since I have seen a fire in my room excepting the blaze of the candle, and that only when, on account of economy, I do not go to bed at twilight."

So saying Ternisien took a chair and seating himself without ceremony, totally forgetful of manners, extended his feet on the fender, while, with his two elbows resting on his knees, he stretched out his meagre and wrinkled hands toward the fire.

Julius Valabert, who found his professor as he had left him, simple and full of kindness, was gazing at him with true pleasure.

"Poor Ternisien!" he said to him. "I see that you have not been happy, but as you remember me, why have you not called on me? In every case, you would have been kindly received."

"Yes, perhaps I was wrong; but you, used to riches, know one side of almsgiving. To give when one wishes it and can afford it, is very easy, but to ask is more difficult."

"After all, I thank chance that has at last united us again. Here is some work for a few weeks, and I hope you will not refuse that I shall fix the price myself."

"We will fix it together. The little talent which I have is completely at your disposal."

"You, perhaps, live near here, as I had ordered that before looking elsewhere they should search in our ward."

"Yes, I live in a little room at No. 4 Furstemberg street."

Ternisien did not perceive the profound impression his answer produced on Julius and his wife. A pause of a few minutes followed, taking advantage of which Valabert and Adele, in whom these words had awakened the same remembrances, exchange between themselves furtive glances.

"Let us see, Mr. Julius, how I can serve you."

Valabert placed before the eyes of Ternisien a file of papers which were to be copied. Having agreed upon the price, Ternisien was ready to depart, but Julius detained him. He feared to question him, and at the same time he wished that he would speak. These two words "Furstemberg street," resounded in his ears. If his wife had been absent, he would have directly questioned his old professor, who lodging in the same house where he had ceased to go, would perhaps been able to explain what to him had remained a mystery. The presence of Adele, who seemed very little disposed to leave, obliged him to take a round-about turn of words.

"What have you followed during the last few years?"

"A trade which did not suit me," answered Ternisien. "I had lost my professorship at the University, my pupils had left me, although I was still capable of teaching. Certainly my hand was heavier, but the principles, you know well, were good, and experience supplies the lack of the happy liveliness of youth. However, all this was of no use; I was obliged to resign and become a public writer. For some years I worked dissatisfiedly with my vocation. Often I had the intention of giving it up. A circumstance which, in spite of myself, poisoned my conscience: a letter that I had the weakness to copy for a miserable recompense, decided me."

"A letter?" asked Julius with indifference.

"Yes, an anonymous letter which contained very heavy accusations. First of all, you must know that I always nourished a profound contempt for all denunciations of that kind which one has not the courage to sign, and it seemed to me that truth ought not to have any fear of expressing itself openly. Is not this your opinion also, Mr. Julius?"

"Yes," answered he, who, entirely absorbed in Ternisien's narration, no longer observed his wife, and continued:

"How could that letter have made such an impression on your mind as to put in execution such a resolve?,'

"Because that letter might compromise very much and perhaps even kill an innocent person as well, as it denounced a great perfidy."

"Why, then," interrupted Mrs. Valabert, who from the face of her husband had guessed what kind of feelings he was endeavoring to conceal, "why did you not accept the second supposition, which was as probable as the first one?"

Ternisien raised his eyes to the sky and heaved a deep sigh

"You are right, madam, *then* I could, but *to day*——"

"To-day?" repeated Julius.

"I cannot any more. My fear was a presentiment. Alas! it was soon realized in the most painful and cruel manner."

"Of whom did that letter speak?"

"Of a young lady."

"And to whom it was addressed?"

"I was never able to learn. The boy who brought the letter to be copied had orders to have the address written by another hand, and was unwilling to tell me whether he had received these orders from a gentleman or a lady. Such a great mystery troubled me. This was not the first time that I had felt scruples about letters of that sort, but they had never made such an impression upon me, and I reproached myself continually with an action so simple and natural belonging to my vocation, as if I had committed a crime. At that time they were making objections to my remaining any longer in the court of the Holy Chapel. I left the shop and rented, at No. 4 Furstemberg street, a little room vacated by an old woman. The first two nights passed in this, my new lodging, were calm and silent, but in the midst of the third one I was awakened by sighs and smothered moans, and from time to time by distressful cries, the effects of pain. The following day it was said to me that the little apartment near the room I occupied was inhabited by a young lady, at the point of death.

"A few days had passed when one day, returning home at about three o'clock, I was surprised to see the door of the same apartment wide open. I looked into the first room,—nobody was there,—no one in the second,—everywhere the same dreadful silence. I entered the last room, and there, lying insensible on her bed, I saw a young woman whose features, although altered by protracted illness, showed that she must have been beautiful when she was happy.

"I followed the first impulse of pity. I replaced on the pillow the head which hang off the bed. I caused her to inhale from a smelling bottle which I found on the mantel and tried to restore her to consciousness. When she opened her eyes, ashamed to be alone in a room with a young woman, I apologized and hurriedly retired. The porter, whom I questioned, told me that on the same day her servant had left her. Without inquiring what were her means, I ran for and brought with me a nurse to watch over her. Happily, there was some gold in her house. Miss Fanny Dusmenil was her name; I had forgotten to mention it before."

At these words Julius rose. Ternisien, interrupting

his narrative, saw him, pale, subdued, and his face wet with tears. Julius turned toward his wife, and seeing her trembling with a profound grief, pictured in her face, going near to her, took her hand saying:

"Adele, my tears, which were flowing without my own will, are no offense to you. Please retire to your apartments, I entreat you and forgive me."

She lowered her head and went away, saying in a low voice, but with an energetic tone of despair:

"Well, I know that you yet love her."

Ternisien had risen completely dumfounded and when, after the scene which had taken place, he found himself alone with Julius, he not longer knew whether he ought to remain silent or to continue. Valabert, now free from restraint, came to him and inquired:

"Is she dead? Is it true?"

"Yes."

"And her child?"

"Dead also, before the mother. But how do you know?"

"I know; what matters the rest to you? And tell me, was she calumniated?"

"Yes."

"Who told you?"

"Herself, and then I have other irrefutable proof."

"What is it?"

"Listen. Often, in day time, I used to inquire about her health. Her agony lasted long and I had time to win her confidence. I used to pass days and nights at her bedside, and cared for her as if I had been her father. She narrated to me her story. She told me how, on the day preceding her marriage, her lover had come like a raging maniac; how, crediting an anonymous letter, he had accused her. Fancy my surprise and consternation when handing me that letter, I recognized the one I had copied. She swore that notwithstanding appearances which seemed to condemn her, she was innocent; and I, who had a wrong to repair, hastened to ask the name of him who had been deceived by such infamous denunciation, and who would probably have time to acknowledge and repair his fault. She obstinately refused to tell it. 'I wish,' she said, 'that this fearful misfortune might have been delayed a few months, that my child could have been borne alive, and then I would have forced myself to beg in his behalf the pity of the father; but now I am alone and near to death, of what use it will be to importune him? Although for me, who loved him so much, his forgetfulness may be painful, I prefer let him forget, rather than perhaps to awaken in him a useless remorse by letting him know how I am dying.' Her strenght visibly left her. One evening the nurse and I were at her bedside awaiting the fatal moment. For more than an hour she had not spoken. I have always retained the minutest details of that last evening, and a common and childish fact, to which death has imparted a lugubrious and dreadful character, will never be blotted from my memory. Near the head of the table a candle was burning. I tried to increase the light, but as my eyes were darkened with tears and my hand trembled, I extinguished the candle and we were plunged into darkness. 'It is perhaps, the eternal night,' she uttered with feeble voice. These were the last words she pronounced."

Julius had hidden his face in his hands and tears flowed through his fingers. Suddenly, as if he would have kept a doubt for his only excuse, he approached Ternisien and said to him:

"You told me that they had calumniated her, but you did not give me the proof, which you say is irrefutable."

"She had already justified herself of having received a

young man. What condemned her was a ring which she was accused of having given as a love token to her suitor. How it had disappeared she was not able to explain. Well, it had been stolen by her servant, a certain Marion, bribed with gold to steal this ring from the *secretaire*. The same day that for the first time, I entered Fanny's room, Marion, owerpowered by remorse, had gone, after having made a confession of the crime without naming the person who had induced her to commit it. She had placed such a written confession on the bed of her mistress while she was asleep, not having had the courage to accuse herself or to ask forgiveness Fanny refused to search for her. Reading this letter, she had fainted, alone, without help, and chance brought me there and happen to see that confession."

"Enough, enough!" said Julius, " I received that anonymous letter. Fanny is dead,—I murdered her. Who then, around me, has plotted such a barbarous scheme? Did Fanny confided it to you?"

"She named no one. She only spoke to me of propositions made to her by a friend of her lover's family."

"Saint-Gilles! Ah! him, him!—my mother's confidant! Must I believe that they acted in concert, and that after having given her consent to it?———Oh! no, no! he acted alone. Now I remember what he used to tell me. Him him alone, I accuse."

"If you were calmer," said Ternisien, "I would give you the proof you need—the copy of the letter."

"Have you it?"

"I have kept it. The boy who brought it to me had received the order to destroy it, but as he did not know how to read, I, instead of the copy, tore up another piece of paper, without his noticing his substitution. This copy must be at home."

"To-morrow you will bring it to me; no, even to night —now—I need it. Let us go!"

Noticing the convulsive joy which spread over the features of Julius, Ternisien repented of having confided such a thing to him.

"It is difficult to find it immediately, it is necessary that I should search for it. Perhaps it exist no longer. However, by no means will I give it to you unless you first tell me for what purpose you intend to use it."

"I would have a proof, nothing else." replied Julius, "a proof which would give to me the right to spurn the author of that letter."

"All right; I shall leave you now, and to morrow will bring it to you. I hope to find it."

Evening had arrived. Ternisien took leave of Julius and returned to his room very much confused. He had no trouble in finding the letter. He thought it right to take precautions against the youth's anger, and his peaceful character made him believe contempt to be a sufficient vengeance. Valabert, who could not believe in such simplicity, exclaimed:

"He will not give me this proof, but do I really need it."

An hour afterward, a servant went out from his palace with three letters. Two of them were addressed to friends of Julius, the third to Saint-Gilles.

VI.

THE REVERSE OF THE CARDS.

Nearly twenty minutes after Ternisien had entered his room, he heard a knock at his door. This noise interrupted the search he was already making among a bundle of papers to find the autograph he had promised to Julius the following day. As he did not expect visitors, and as in his pre-occupation he had not heard the front door shut, so at first he thought the noise was caused by the wind swinging an open window in the stairway, and, therefore, without further notice, he pursued his work. After a moment, he thought he heard a friction which ascended and descended along the door as if produced by a hand which searched in the darkness for the string of a bell, a thing completely unknown among Ternisien's furniture.

The knocking was repeated a little stronger and with greater energy.

"Who is there and what do you want?" asked Ternisien. He received no answer, but the knocking was repeated.

"Come again to-morrow," said the good man, alarmed at such persistency, and fearing to be the victim of some snare. "Come again to-morrow; I am already in bed and have no light."

Unhappily, the candle, the light of which was seen through the cracks of his door, belied his words.

"Open the door, please," asked a sweet and trembling voice; "you have nothing to fear from the person speaking to you." Ternisien decided to open the door.

A veiled woman quickly entered the room. She seemed a victim of the greatest agitation, and when she raised her veil to breathe at ease, the old professor uttered an exclamation of surprise on observing the change which a few hours had produced in her features.

"Close the door" said she.

Before obeying, Ternisien cast a glance at the staircase.

"Alone? you are alone, madam!"

"Nobody knows nor ought to know of my visit to your house. Swear to me, sir, that if you should be questioned, you will not reveal that I came here."

"Madam," replied Ternisien, still more amazed by the visit and by the mystery that this lady put in it, "madam, it is not customary for me to pledge myself so easily to such oaths, which sometimes become painful and difficult to keep. When you will have the kindness to explain the causes which brought you here, I will try to make you the promise you ask."

"I understand your prudence, but have no fears, the secret I ask is more necessary to me than to you. Be yourself the judge."

She cast her eyes around the room, and, after a few minutes, added:

"Here we must talk low, must we not? Others can hear what is said."

"Yes, madam, it was in this same room that, without caring for it, I heard the smothered moans of the unhappy Fanny. You were not in the parlor when I finished the narration of that very sad story?"

"Yes, yes," interrupted Adele with an abrupt and agitated tone of voice, "I know that *that* Fanny is dead."

"After my departure M. Valabert had the time to tell you?"

"I have not seen him since."

"Yet he is ignorant that you have come to see me?"

"He is."

"But, madam, if this evening he should discover your absence?"

"This evening?—O, this evening he will not think of what may I have done. Now he does not think of me any more."

In spite of his want of penetration and his absolute ignorance of passion, Ternisien began to guess the secret grief which thus changed the features of Mrs. Valabert, and gave to her eyes that insane expression and to her voice that strange inflection. He recollected the tears Valabert had not been able to hide from her, and with what words he had entreated her to retire. Jealousy was gnawing her heart, but he could not yet guess the motive which had brought her to his lodgings.

She motioned him to sit down beside her.

"Have you kept the copy of that anonymous letter?"

Ternisien stared at her with astonishment, not knowing whether she was questioning, or affirming a fact well known to her.

"You have kept it" she continued; to morrow you are going to give it to my husband. Do not try to deny it; from the next room I heard all, I know all. Even when your voice or his had not reached me, my gaze would have pierced through the thickness of the walls and guessed your words from the simple movement of your lips. You must give me the copy of that letter."

"Madam, I promised to give it to your husband."

"To him or to me, what matters it to you?"

"If you are here with his consent."

"To-morrow you will write him that you have lost that paper, and he will believe it. Have you not already made its existence doubtful?"

"Indeed, I fear I have told the truth."

"No; at the beginning you quite assented that it was yet in your hands, and you have begun the search. I will have that copy. Give it to me, sir; sell it to me, ask for it whatever price you will; you are poor and I can enrich you."

Speaking so rapidly as not to leave him time to answer she had opened her satchel.

Then she added: "Here are four bills of a thousand francs each; these are not enough?—I know it—this is what I had in the casket. I will give you more, much more; I will treble the sum—twenty thousands francs—and I have jewels—here, take."

Her color, before pale, had returned, her hands with a movement so rapid as hardly to be followed by the eyes, emptied the satchel. A pearl necklace, precious stones, diamonds, rings, her own ear-rings, in a twinkling of an eye, were thrown upon the knees of Ternisien.

The poor man, astounded, contemplated her. On the flaps of his ragged coat was a sum tenfold larger than he had before possessed in all his life-time, and this unexpected fortune was given him without reckoning; yes it was his own. It was enough that he should extend his arm and shut his hands to become the master of it. But such were not the thoughts in Ternisien's mind. Between the wealth he had never known and the misery which was shortening his life, in that honest heart was no place for speculation, however excusable it may be. With trembling voice and tears in his eyes, he addressed Mrs. Valabert.

"Are you then very unhappy?"

"Yes, very unhappy," she answered, "and it is in your power that I may be so no longer; you can give me peace and insure my happiness. Do you accept it then?"

"The recital of that story has awakened in your husband

the remembrance of a former love. Is it not true? I ought to have perceived this and broken it off when he entreated you to go out of the room; I ought not to have re-opened a wound yet unhealed. You must forgive me, madam, the evil that I have unwittingly done you. I had present in my memory the death of that poor woman, who was an angel of virtue—I could swear it,—and who has been so basely calumniated. If you had know her as I did, if you had heard her protest her innocence, you would not have required this irrefutable proof to have been convinced of it. But forgive me, madam, if I again afflict you in speaking of her, and forget what I learned but a few minutes ago, namely, that love is jealous of a rival who does not even exist any more. You are afraid that your husband would become attached to that souvenir, and that at your side he would remember her whom he loved. How the possession of that letter could make you happy is what I am not able to understand. What interest causes you to wish so ardently for it as to be ready to purchase it with you own fortune?"

Whether Adele had not a satisfactory answer ready or whether the emotion by which she was agitated was too strong, she remained silent.

Ternisien continued:

"When I saw that Mr. Julius wished for that letter, I immediately told him that perhaps it would be impossible for me to find it, because I was afraid that, recognizing the handwriting, he would have gone to ask satisfaction of him who had written it. He has re-assured me. What ought I to suppose, now that I see you troubled by such a fear?"

"Well, yes, I fear that he may expose his life," answered Adele, as if the last words of Ternisien had given her the excuse she had been searching for. "Your friendship for him has surmised the misfortune which my love tries to prevent. That is why I come here at this late hour, and why I beg you not to speak to any one of my visit. I know,—do not ask how I know,—the person who wrote that letter; my husband, too, will recognize the handwriting; they will fight, be sure of it; perhaps he will be killed.—Twice I will lose him on account of that unhappy woman. Give me that letter—let me destroy that proof—and when he has only suspicions; when the guilty one is able to deny, and, therefore, to refuse to fight, then I will be happy or at least at ease about my husband's life. This letter, I ask for it upon my knees."

"Rise, madam," said Ternisien. "I am too sorry for what has happened not to give you back your tranquillity. The oath you ask from me, I give you willingly. I will hide your visit from Mr. Valabert, but take this money again, take back these jewels; I will not accept them. In returning you this letter, I intend only to repair a wrong done and not to give you back a proof."

In so speaking, Ternisien returned to Mrs. Valabert the bills and jewels she had handed him. He went to the table on which some papers were scattered, searched a little and afterward returned towards Adele. Seeing the yellow paper he had in his hands, she sprang and seized it with a convulsive movement. While she was reading, a strange change was taking place in her, a change which only the wish to prevent a challenge by destroying that proof could not justify to eyes more expert than those of Ternisien. In her joy was something of frenzy. One would have said that of the two opposite natures existing in her, the most violent—for a long time bridled by an iron will—had finally burst forth and removed all obstacles —overflowed by her violent passions. Her features, the mirror of a new soul, seemed to have assumed another character. She was no more the timid, submitting resigned, suppliant woman, but a lioness which roared while devouring her prey. As if her hands were not sufficient, she tore the sheet with her teeth, and then, gathering up the pieces, burned them in the flame of the candle, one by one. In proportion as they were consumed, her eyes shone and followed the writhings of the flame as if they were the sufferings of an agonized victim. As soon as the fire had devoured all, she dispersed the blackened ashes which flew around her with a puff.

"Nothing more" she cried. "Behold every trace has disappeared! This letter never existed. I am saved!"

In her delirious joy, she twisted her hands, laughing and crying at same time. She threw herself upon the neck of Ternisien before he was able to express his wonder at such unaccountable exuberance.

"To you I owe my happiness," she replied; "I will never forget it. You refuse my gifts but come to see me, sir; as I have told you, my fortune is yours. I have your own word that you will be discreet: is it not so? Good-bye. Do not accompany me; I will find my way. The important thing is that I do not stay here any longer."

She opened the door, rushed to the staircase, and despite the darkness, so nimble were her steps that Ternisien scarcely heard the noise. The street door was shut, Ternisien placed himself at the window and by the uncertain light of a street lamp saw her turning a corner through the snow.

For some time the old professor remained thunderstruck at what had happened. A thousand different ideas whirled in his poor head. The thought of evil was the last one which could enter his mind, but, upon thinking of the offers he had refused, it seemed to him that if he had accepted them it would have been a heavy burden on his conscience, and that he would have been obliged to return the gifts. He wrote to Mr. Valabert that all his researches had been useless; that for a long time he had kept that paper, but that it existed no longer. Then he went to bed, but was unable to sleep or to banish the suspicions which incessantly presented themselves to his mind.

Mrs. Valabert had returned home without having been even inquired for by her husband in her absence. During the night, no noise troubled the quietness of the house. At dawn the following morning, Julius aroused from the table where he had spent the whole night in writing. He re-read and sealed some letters. A very long one was addressed to his wife; another also of several pages contained his last dispositions, and was to be given to the notary who had his fortune.

His wife's room was separated from his own by a smaller one, the door of which opened between the two divisions of the library. He directed his steps to that side, and listened for a few minutes. All around was still " She is asleep," he said; " I can go out, and if Heaven is just I shall return here without troubling her rest. In two hours all will be ended. He or I. Let me go." He wrapped himself in a cloak, took the box which contained his pistols, and softy turned the key in the lock.

At the same time, the door opened from the outside and Julius found himself face to face with his wife who was pale, troubled and with a countenance which testified that she, too, had been awake all night.

Surprise made Julius draw back. Adele entered, shut the cabinet door violently and, without asking or giving explanations, took away the cloak and snatched the pistol box from her husband's hands.

" You were going out to fight," she said.

Julius scarcely recovered from his emotion, replied:

"I must be second for a friend. These pistols are for him. Adele, do not be afraid, but let me go."

"Oh! you cannot deceive me," she said; "you are going to fight."

"Adele!"

"No useless words! no false oaths! You go to fight."

"To fight? Why? and against whom?"

Against whom? Against him who wrote that anonymous letter and whom you think you know. Why? Because you wish to avenge the death of whom you always thought. I know it, I tell you. Does the heart need to be taught that is forsaken? Does the jealousy need to be enlightened? Did I not see you yesterday, while that man was speaking, forget that I was there,—I, a poor, forsaken woman,—and only recollect it to pray me not to trouble your grief with my presence? And because I retired you thought I had not heard your sobs, or the questions you asked, or the resolution you made? Julius, dare you repeat to me that you are not going to fight?"

He turned his eyes toward her, and making an effort, he replied with a grave and slow voice: Adele, it has always been my sad fate to put to a trial your inexaustible kindness, which made an angel of you. Once you alone rendered justice to that woman whom you now detest on account of the title of my wife. Later, when I was very near dying, you again consoled me; for almost two years you sorrounded me with attentions, and I swear to you, without that unforeseen revelation which threw me suddenly into the past, no moaning or sorrow, or remembrance would have found place in my heart. Try to find in that virtue which no other woman equally possesses, the necessary strenght to bear this last blow. Yes, I will no longer deceive you. I go to fight. It is not a question of love, as no vengeance can give life again to her who no longer exists, but the infamous person who calumniated the woman you yourself once defended, must receive the price of his falsehood. To-day, to-morrow, twenty years from now, so long as my hand can hold a sword or direct a ball through the heart of an adversary, I will demand satisfaction for that vile conduct; I will, avenge Fanny's death. I wished to avoid meeting you, Adele; I feared your tears, your pains, your reproaches, but my last thoughts were for you. There, on the mantel piece, is a letter I wrote you, in which I bade you the last farewell. Receive it now, since a fatal chance has brought you across my path, and do not try to detain me. My resolution is taken. It is a reparation that I owe her; and in risking my life, I expiate, in my opinion, my credulity and the error I ought to have repulsed far from me."

Adele had remained before him dumb, with a fixed gaze and clasped hands, but when she saw that he again prepared to leave, she seized him violently by the arm, and exclaimed with an accent of subdued rage:

"Then I must again resign myself to be patient? This everlasting duty! For others, the passion, the heart which burns and confides itself,— for me the coldness of marble. No, no! this must not be so! He asks me for another virtue, while I—O God! I beg thee to restrain the passion which was ready to overflow. Let not the secret of my heart come to my lips. Seal my mouth, and restrain my voice before it shall narrate what I know. Let this blindness which betrays me depart from me, and give me back my former strong will."

"Adele, what do you mean to say?" asked Julius, "Whence this delirium?"

"Must I even explain to you the cause of my grief?

Do you thing to deceive me? Was that woman, then so beautiful that the simple remembrance of her is stronger than your love for me? In what way she loved, to love you more than I do? You do not know, Julius, how, I love you. You have only known in me a timid, reserved woman, whom a simple glance was sufficient to make happy, but I was waiting only for a single impassioned word, for a worm caress, to attach myself to you, to love you—not as a wife, but as a lover. Oh! tell me that you were ignorant of these transports, of these secret desires, of that love which dare not to burst forth, but which to-day made me fall at your feet, confounded, suppliant, mad? Is it not so? You will forget that woman for me, who entreats; who, crying, kisses your hands, your knees. Yes, she was beautiful; but I ?—I, too, am beautiful; you have told me so too often to ignore it, and happiness will make me yet more beautiful; and you will look at me with pride. Yes, she was innocent; and, am I guilty in loving you? As she died, I will die too, if you forsake me. Do you then desire to kill us both?"

Julius was moved, but not persuaded. He felt how legitimate was Adele's sorrow, and how strong, to cause her to speak in such an infatuated way, so destitute of modesty. Her words affected his ears, not his heart,—since the preceding day his heart had been wholly absorbed in the remembrance of Fanny. Freeing himself from his wife, he made a few steps, as if to go out.

"So you *will* go, you *will* leave me? all that I have said has been useless to detain you?"

"I *must* go."

"You will not return here unless avenged or dead!"

"Rightly!"

"And during your absence I, who know all, will cry, tear my hair, strike my forehead against the wall—and all that cannot detain you? On the field, facing your adversary, nothing can affect you? nothing will prevent your heart beating or your hand trembling? This is what is in store for me: You, if you come back, will return to cry for her beside me, or be brought here a corpse, or dying, and I shall cure you and restore your life to hear you repeat the name of Fanny. Oh! see, Julius, do you know that you will drive me mad? that I would prefer to see you dead rather than alive? But you will not depart from hence—you will not fight.—Who is your adversary? Who killed your beloved? Saint-Gilles; it is not so?"

"Who else could have done it?"

"And if he refuses to fight?"

"He will not refuse; I have his answer already."

"His answer to an insulting letter. Yet one does not risk his life for an insult that could be repaired. If he refuses to fight; if he tells you that he did not write that letter?"

I will tell him that he is a coward; I will take him by the throat with one hand and with the other I will slap his face."

"But then perhaps, he will kill you; and yet—he did not write that letter."

"Who did then?"

"Some one that you cannot strike—some one that does not wish for your death."

"Adele!"

"Some one who embraces your feet; a woman whom jealousy made guilty, and who speaks now on account of the fear of losing you. It was I Julius."

"You?"

At such a fearful revelation, Julius remained as if striken by a thunderbolt.

"*You*" he repeated after a few minutes.

": Yes, I," she answered, trying to seize his hands, which he drew back. He was looking at her with amazement and terror. He was taken with dizziness in measuring that profound falsity and the abysses of that heart, —a burning volcano covered with snow. Finally he exclaimed: " What had that poor thing done to you? Oh! if you have spoken the truth, do not approach me henceforth. I would feel only pity for you, but you excite my horror."

"Julius, you ask what she had done to me? But I loved you from the first day I saw you, and she also loved you. Do not ask me how I happened to be acquainted with Ernest's visits. I was jealous, and gold bought me all the secrets I wished to know. It was I that caused the letter to be copied with all the precautions Ternisien narrated. Yesterday I received from him and burned the paper written by my hand. I bought Marion, and for me she stole the ring whose disappearance was to serve as a proof against Fanny. That is what I did, and it seems a dream. I cannot believe it myself. My reason is wandering, my head is feeble as my body.—Why have I spoken? Oh! yes, I remember, because you were going to fight with Saint-Gilles; because you were going to risk your life and I desired to save you."

"Have you yet that ring which Marion gave you? Answer, answer! Give it to me."

" I have it no more."

" Give it to me!" he repeated with a fearful voice.

"Julius" she replied, I have it no more. Your looks affright me; your voice makes me tremble. Have you no pity for me?"

"Had you pity for her?"

"Always HER!"

"Do you not remember that she is dead, and died murdered by you? Pity for you? Never!"

"I, too, have suffered. Was I not jealous? Am I not yet so? Have I not suffered when victim of a love which could cause me to lose all modesty, I saw you going out to meet her? Have I not silently concealed my tears? Have I not sighed every night? Mute and impassible in appearance, have I not staggered at the noise of your footsteps, at the sound of your voice, and when your hand touched mine? And during two years what has been my lot? By day Fanny occupies your thoughts, and often even at night in your dreams I have heard her name. Did I complain? And to-day, because the fear of losing you has made me speak, fool that I was, you reject me without pity. Your eyes have not a single tear for my sufferings, your heart has not an excuse for my fault. She could have died; she! you had loved her. What would become of me if you will not see me any more? A word only for pity; not a word of love. Now you cannot speak it; I know it, and you would make me so happy. No, no! it is not that which I ask of you. Only let fall a look upon me as formerly, as yesterday, and I will leave you in peace. You will think of her, you will cry for her, and I—when your eyes shall be dry, I will return to you, I will kneel and ask your pardon. Oh! my head burns. A word, only a word, or I shall die!"

She had approached him; he pushed her back again.

"Infamous one!" he exclaimed, "if you yet have it, give me that ring."

"What will you do with it?" she asked raising her head and regaining an energy inspired by despair.

"I would in your presence cover it with kisses and let you know once again, before we part, how I love her who had it."

"To part? Oh! Julius, you defy me? You believe me feeble and under your feet. To separate? But I am your wife and will follow you everywhere. What will you say to obtain that separation? That for jealousy I murdered your mistress? And the proof where is it? That letter was destroyed. I will answer that you were lying. Ah! you are without pity for me; you will punish me for my love for you with the remembrance you retain of the other and then forsake me. Well, then! As your wife I claim my right to remain with you; I will never leave. Do you understand?"

"Madam, we shall not see each other again."

"We will see each other every day. Every day I will importune you with my presence, with my love, with my distress and my jealousies."

"Be silent, madam, be silent!"

"No, I will not; neither to-day nor to morrow. Ah! you believe to have suffered by having lost your darling while another woman whose reason you have destroyed only receives from you the epithet of infamous and the threat of a separation. No, no! We are united to each other, and we will not be parted. Our existence will be a hell, but I am used to suffering, and I accept my lot."

Out of her mind, almost mad she had taken the arm of her husband, whose rage had been increased by such foolish provocation. A fearful expression of contempt and hatred shone in his eyes. The door of the room opened with violence, and at the same time three gentlemen entered. Julius made a last effort, and as he had not seen the presence of the others, raised his hand against his wife. She bent and fell, half fainting under the blow.

"Gentlemen," said he, "the hour I appointed for our meeting is past. Without doubt you come to search for me. Mr. Saint-Gilles, I would not have delayed presenting my excuses to you and praying to forget the letter I had addressed you. You can see the motive of my delay, a conjugal scene, that I cannot hide like the others. Madam was asking for a separation which I was refusing to her; now I do not object any longer, and the testimony you will make in her favor will be the punishment of a brutality of which I feel ashamed, but of which it is too late now to repent."

He approached his wife, and in a low voice said to her:

"To day you will lodge your complaint, otherwise before these gentlemen I will dishonor you by telling what I know."

EPILOGUE.

A month after that scene Julius and Adele were separated. Two month later Julius mourned his wife, and the year was not ended when Ternisien in tears accompanied a funeral retinue that went out from the palace of the *Rue de Lille*.

POEMS

TRANSLATED FROM

French, Italian, and Spanish.

———

THIRD EDITION.

I.

ON THE DEATH OF A GIRL.

TO MY BELOVED MOTHER, FORTUNATA SORVILLO, WIDOW NOBILE, (NEE NANSÒ).

Twelve springs had embellished her youth. Poor girl! she could have lived longer. To her eyes the future was opening full of delight, and her beautiful smile was pure as a golden ray of the sun.

The life of this beloved one was the support of her mother's soul. Innocence supports, while virtue defends. She was used to say, "This angel, one day, will become a woman," and this child was the living incarnation of her happiness.

And thou hast lived twelve years embellishing all on thy passage, for twelve years thy mother found her bliss in the looks of thy charming eyes; for twelve years she had in her soul a continual happiness knowing that thou wast living.

On the storm of life this girl was a calm, and in sorrows was a ray of dawn, and thou, alas! suddenly left us, leaving in our heart an everlasting sadness.

Her soul was the human embodiment of the virtues,—the virtues, flowers of heaven, and perfumes of the elect. Afterward a child was needed in the bands of the angels, God* singled her out, Death came, and she was no more.

The mother thoughtful, dishevelled, stayed there to look at the body, mute for ever. Alas! for a moment it

---

*God wanted one more angel child,
  Amidst His shining band,
And so He reached, with loving smile,
  And clasped our darling's hand!

seemed that her life had disappeared with that of the poor girl for whom the funeral bell was tolling. Oh! I seem still to see this girl with her rigid, silent form, and her pale face! Oh! I see her cold and beautiful, lying in the bed as she were sleeping in an angelic dream.

I see the light around her shed its reddish lustre in the humble and sad room. I yet see the friendly hand faithful to its duty, raise up and place her corpse in the coffin. O! when this little body was brought to the churchyard, the mother groaned for her lost happiness. One would have said that her heart wished to follow the coffin, so many were the sobs which poured from her oppressed breast. The day was over, and gave place to another,— and yet the mother has always in her heart her daughter, and seems always to see her angel prostrated by death.

Vainly she is invited to many joyful feasts,—vain it is to persuade her of the necessity of forgetting,—vainly it is said that life has the same law for all, and that, by death, hearts are united to God.

Vainly it is repeated to her that the flowers live only a season; that the beautiful dawn which awokes the morning cannot continue; that the children's souls, up in Heaven, live again, and at our own death they show themselves to us.

The poor mother remains deaf to all these words. In vain every one tells her that her daughter is an angel,— that Death must extend its law over all,—that life is an exile in this world,—that all must change. Alas! her heart is broken,—her faith is extinguished. The mother cannot, and will not believe that she is dead; and continually with her tears asks for her daughter. She demands this girl, who still lives in her mind, with her songs, with her games, and with her gay smile. Sometimes her mind wanders for a moment, and it seems that her soul has risen to the clouds to see if her time had arrived to depart far away from the noise.—Thus she lives amidst our human shadows, always faithful to her daughter,—her dearest love. Many weeks I have heard her cry, and since I have been told, that she is still weeping.

Brasseur.

II.

THE NIGHT OF OCTOBER.

TO MY BROTHER, CAV. GIOVANNI SORVILLO.

POET.

The pain I suffered has vanished like a dream, and the faint remembrance it has left I can only compare to those mists which rise with the dawn and disperse with the dew.

MUSE.

What ailed thee, my poet, and what was the pain that parted thee from me? Alas! I yet felt its sad effects. What is this unknown grief I have so long bevailed?

POET.

It was a vulgar pain, well known to man, but when our heart is grieved, we always believe, poor fools that we are, that nobody before us has known sorrow.

MUSE.

Only the sorrow of a vulgar mind can be called vulgar. Friend, reveal this sad misery of thy heart; believe me; speak with confidence. The severe God of silence is one of the brethren of death; complaint brings consolation, and often a single word has spared remorse.

POET.

If I were to speak of my pain, truly I shall not know by what name to call it,—if it be love, folly, pride, experience, or if it could be of profit to anybody—but as we are now alone, seated by the fire, I will tell my story. Take thy lyre and let my memory awaken at the sound of thy notes.

MUSE.

Before relating thy sorrows, Poet, art thou cured? Think, that to-day thou must speak without love or hatred; recollect that I have received the sweet name of consoler, and make me not the accomplice of the passions that have ruined thee.

POET.

I am so well cured of my malady, that sometimes I doubt if it ever existed; and where I risked my existence, instead of myself, I fancy I see the face of a stranger. Muse, be without fear, we may both without danger confide in the voice of thy inspiration. It is sweet to smile at the remembrance of ills we might have forgotten.

MUSE.

Like a watchful mother at the cradle of a beloved child, I trembling turn to thy heart which was closed to me. Speak, friend, my attentive lyre already follows the accents of thy voice, and in a ray of light, like a beautiful vision, pass by the shades of other days.

POET.

Days of work, the only days in which I really lived. Oh, solitude thrice beloved! God be praised, at last I have returned to my old study! Poor room, walls so often deserted, dusty chairs, faithful lamp! Oh, my palace, my little world, and thou young immortal Muse, God be praised, we are again going to sing! Yes, I will open my soul, thou shalt know all, and I will relate thee the ills that a woman can do,—for a woman it was, my poor friend, (alas! perhaps thou already knowest it,) a woman to whom I submitted as a serf submits to his master. Detested yoke, it was there my heart lost its force and its youth, and yet near my mistress I had fancied I should find happiness. When in the evening near the brook we walked togheter on the silvery sand, when the white specter of the poplar showed us the road from afar, I can yet see by the ray of the moon, her beautiful frame leaning on my arm. Let us speak no more of it. I did not foresee where fortune would lead me; doubtless the anger of the Gods had needed a victim, for my attempt to be happy has been punished as a crime.

MUSE.

The image of a sweet remembrance has just presented itself to thy thoughts. Why fearest thou to retrace its track? Young man if fortune has been cruel, do like her, smile on thy first love.

POET.

No, it is at my misfortune that I have acquired the right to smile. Muse, I said I would without passion relate my sorrows, my dreams, my madness, and that I would tell thee the time, the hour, and the occasion. It was, I recollect, a night of autumn, sad and cold, like to-night; the murmur of the wind with monotonous noise nursed dark cares in my troubled mind. I was at the window, expecting my mistress, and listening in the obscurity, I felt such a distress in my heart, that I conceived the suspicion of an infidelity. The street where I lodged was dark and deserted; some shadows passed a lantern in their hands. When the wind whistled in the half closed door one heard in the distance what seemed a human sigh. I know not—to say the truth—to what sad presentiment my restless spirit then abandoned itself. I recalled in vain the remains of my courage, and I felt a tremor when I hear the clock strike. She came not. Alone with downcast eyes I looked anxiously at the walls and the road; and I have not told thee what a senseless ardor that inconstant woman lighted in my bosom. Her alone I loved in the world, and to live a day without her seemed to me a destiny more dreadful than death; still I remember in that fearful night I make a long effort to break my chain. A hundred times I called her perfidious and false. I reminded myself of all the ills she had caused me. Alas! at the recollection of her fatal beauty what ills, what griefs were still unappeased? At length the day broke. Tired with vain expectation, I fell into a slumber on the rails of the balcony. I opened my eyes at the rising dawn, and let my dazzled orbs wander around me. Suddenly at a turning of a narrow lane I heard on the gravel stealthy footsteps. It is she. She enters. Whence comest thou? Last night what hast thou done? answer, what would'st thou? What brings thee at this hour? Whilst I alone on this balcony watch and weep, in what place, to whom did'st thou smile? Perfidious, audacious woman, is it possible thou come to me? What askest thou? By what horrible thirst darest thou seek to draw me to thy exhausted arms? Go, retire, spectre of my beloved—return to the grave if thou art risen from it—leave me to forget forever the joy of my youth, and when I think of thee to believe that I have dreamed.

MUSE.

Calm thyself; I conjure thee. Thy words make me shudder; thy wound is near to re-open. Alas! it is very deep, and the miseries of this world are so long ere they are effaced. Forget, my child, and from thy heart drive the name of that woman I will not pronounce.

POET.

Shame to thee who first taught me treachery, and maddened me with horror and rage. Shame to thee woman of the dark eyes, whose fatal love buried in the shade my spring and my bright days. Thy voice, thy smiles, thy corrupting glances taught me to curse even the appearance of happiness: thy youth, thy charms reduced me to despair, and if I no longer believe in tears it is because I see thee weep. Shame on thee! I was as simple as a child; like a flower at the dawn my heart opened to thy love—sure that heart without defense could easily be abused—but to leave it its innocence was still easier. Shame on thee! Thou wast the mother of my first sorrows, and thou caused'st a fountain of tears to flow from my eyes—yet it flows and nothing will ever heal it, but in that bitter source I will bathe, and I shall forget, I hope, thy abhorred remembrance.

MUSE.

Poet; it is enough. Though the illusions with the faithless one lasted but a day, do not curse that day when thou speakest of her—if thou desirest to be loved, respect thy love—if the effort is too great for human weakness to pardon the ills that come to us from others, spare thyself at least the torments of hatred, and, in default of pardon, let oblivion come. The dead sleep in peace in the bosom of the heart; and thus should sleep the feelings which are extinguished; the relics of the heart have also their ashes. Do not let our hands touch these sacred remains. Why in this narration of a vivid suffering, wilt thou only see a dream and a deluded love? Does Providence act without a motive? or, thinkest thou that the God who struck thee, struck inadvertently? The blow of which thou complainest has, perhaps, saved thee, child, by that thy heart was opened. Man is an apprentice, and sorrow is his master, and no one knows himself until he has suffered. Hard is the law, but supreme, old as the world and the fate, that we must receive the baptism of misfortune, and at such sad price everything must be bought. The crops to ripen have need of dew. The symbol of joy is a broken plant wet with rain and covered with flowers. Did'st thou not say that thou wast cured of thy folly? Art thou not young, fortunate, well received by all—and those light pleasures which make life desirable—what would'st thou care for them, if thou had'st not wept? When on the decline of day, seated on the hearth thou drinkest to liberty, say, would'st thou raise thy glass so heartily if thou had'st not paid the price of thy gayety? Would'st thou love flowers, meadows, the green shade, the sonnets of Petrarch, and the songs of the birds, Michel Angelo and the arts, Shakespear and nature, if thou didst not find some of these old sighs in them? Would'st thou understand the ineffable harmony of the heavens, the silence of the night, the murmur of the waves, if in some other places fever and sleeplessness had not made thee think of eternal rest? Hast thou not now a fair mistress—and, when on going to sleep, thou pressest her hand, the distant recollection of thy youth does not render her divine smile more sweet. Dost thou not walk together in the midst of flowering woods, on the silvery sand and in that palace of verdure? Does the white spectre of the poplar no longer show the road by the ray of the moon? Dost thou not see, as then by the ray of the moon, a beautiful form lean her hand on thy arm—and if in thy path thou shouldst meet with fortune, would'st thou not follow her gaily singing? Of what then dost thou complain? Immortal hope is revived in thee by the hand of misfortune. Oh, my child, pity her, the unfaithful one, who formerly made the tears flow from thy eyes. Wherefore wouldst thou hate the experience of thy youth, and detest an ill which has rendered thee better? Pity her she is a woman and God made thee, when with her, guess by suffering, the secret of happiness. Her task was painful. She, perhaps, loved thee, but destiny willed that she should break thy heart; she knew life, and she made thee know it. Another has culled the fruit of thy sorrow—pity her—her sad love has passed like a dream; she saw thy wound, but could not close it. Her tears were not deceitful, and even though they were, pity her. Thou now knowest how to love.

POET.

Thou speakest truth. Hatred is impious, it is a shuddering, full of horror—when that viper, curled up in our hearts unfolds itself. Hear me then, Goddess, and be witness of my oath.—By the blue eyes of my mistress—by the azure of the firmament—by that brilliant star which bears the name of Venus, and, like a diamond, shines from afar on the horizon—by the tranquil and pure light of the star, dear to the traveler—by the herbs of the prairie—by the forests—by the green meadows—by the powers of life—by the productive force of the universe, I banish you from my memory, remains of an insensate love; mysterious and dark history which sleeps with the past—and thou who formerly hast borne the fame and sweet name of my beloved, the instant I forgot thee forever ought also to be the moment of forgiveness. Let us pardon one another. I break the chain which united us before God With my last tear receive an eternal adieu;

and now, fair dreamer, now, Muse, to our own love—
sing me some joyous song as in the first times of our
bright days. Already the fragrant lawn feels the approach
of the morning. Come to walk my dearest, and to smell
the flowers of the garden; come to see immortal nature
rise from the veil of sleep, we shall revive with her, at the
first ray of the sun.

A. De Musset.

III.

THE NIGHT OF DECEMBER.

TO MY DEAR SISTER JOSEPHINE CALLIGE, (NEE SORVILLO.)

At the time I was a school-boy one evening I remained sitting up in the lonely hall; there came to sit at my table a poor child all dressed in black, who resembled me as a brother. His face was beautiful and sad; by the light of my lamp he came to read in my open book, leaned his forehead on my hand, and smiling, remained thoughtful until the morrow.

When I was fifteen years old I was walking one day with slow steps in a wood. At the foot of a tree a young man dressed in black came to sit, who resembled me as a brother. I asked him my way; in one hand he had a lute, in the other a bunch of roses; he gave me a friendly greeting, and, turning away, with his finger pointed to the hill.

I had reached the age when we believe in love. One day I was alone in my room with the tears of a first sorrow. At my fireside came to sit a stranger, all dressed in black, who resembled me as a brother. He was sad and thoughtful; with one hand he pointed me to heaven, and with the other he held a poniard. It seemed that he suffered from my pains, but he did not sigh, and vanished like a dream.

At the age when man is licentious, one day I raised my glass to drink a toast at a feast; opposite to me come to sit a guest, all dressed in black, who resembled me like a brother. Under his mantle he shook a rag of purple torn to pieces, on his head he had a wild myrtle, his thin arm tried to press mine, and the drinking glass in my feeble hand broke as soon as it touched his.

A year after in the night I was on my knees at the bed where my father had first died, there, at the bedside came and sat an orphan all dressed in black, who resembled me as a brother. His eyes were moistened with tears; like the angel of sorrow he was crowned with thorns, his lute was lying on the ground, his purple was the color of the blood, and his poniard was in his breast.

I recollect him so well that always in every moment of my life I recognized him. It was a strange vision, and, yet, angel or devil, I have seen everywhere his friendly shade.

When later, tired of suffering, I tried to exile myself from France to be born again or to die, when impatient of moving I went in search of the vestige of a hope, at Pisa, to the feet of the Apenines—at Cologne, opposite to Rhine—at Nice, to the declivity of the valley—at Florence, in the midst of palaces—at Brigues, in those old castles in the midst of the desolate Alps—at Geneva, under the cedars—at Vevey under the green apple trees—at Havre, in front of the Atlantic—at Venice, on the arid Lido, where on the grass of a grave has just died the pale Adriatic; everywhere over this immense earth I have wandered, my eyes bleeding from everlasting wounds; everywhere limping weariness, dragging my fatigue after it, has dragged me in a hurdle; everywhere always thirsting for the knowledge of an unknown, I went after the shadow of my dreams; everywhere, without having lived, I have seen what I had already seen, the human face and its illusions; everywhere I wished to live; everywhere I wished to die; everywhere I touched the land, always there came across my path a wretched man, all dressed in black, who resembled me as a brother.

Who art thou, whom in this life I have met in my way? Seeing thee so sad, I cannot believe thee to be my evi' genius; thy sweet smile is full of infinite patience, and thy tears show so great pity. In looking at thee, thy sorrow seems brother to my pain, and resembles friendship.

Who art thou? Surely thou art not my good angel. Never thou comest to advise me. Thou seest my misfortunes, and strange to say, thou indifferently dost let me suffer. For twenty years thou hast walked on my road, and until now I should not know how I ought to call thee. Thou smilest, without partaking of my joy. Thou pitiest me, without bringing me any consolation.

This evening also thou hast appeared to me. The night was chilly. Alone bending on my bed I was looking at a place, yet warm with burning kisses, and was thinking how soon a woman forgets, and feeling a part of my life pine away.

I collected letters of past days, and tresses remains of our love. All this past repeated the eternal oaths of a day. I was looking at these holy relics which made my hand tremble. Tears of my heart, devoured by the heart, and which to-morrow will not be known, even from the eyes which have shed them.

I wrapped in a coarse covering the remains of happier days. Methought that here below what lasts longest is a lock of hair. Like the diver who goes down in a deep sea I lose myself in such forgetfulness. On every side I revolved the probe, and alone far from the eyes of the world I mourned o'er my poor buried love.

Already I was prepared to seal in black those frail and dear treasures. Already I was to restore it, and not being able to believe it, I doubt it. Ah! feeble woman, proud, senseless, in thy spite thou wilt remember me. Why, why liest thou to thy own mind? To what purpose all this weeping, this heaving bosom, these sobs if thou dost not love me?

Yes thou languishest, thou sufferest, thou weepest, but a dark shadow is between us. Well, then, good bye, adieu. Thou wilt count the hours which separate thee from me. Go, go, and in thy cold heart satisfy thy pride. I feel my heart yet young and strong, and many evils could yet find a place among the evils that you have caused me.

Go! go! immortal nature had not endowed thee with all virtues. Ah! poor woman, who would be beautiful and not forgive. Depart, depart, follow thy destiny. I who love thee have not yet lost all. Throw to the winds our exstinguished love. Is it possible? Thou whom I loved so much? If thou wilt go, why lovest thou me?

But suddenly in the darkness of night I see a form cross the room without making any noise. I see a shadow appear on my curtains; it comes and sits on my bed. Who art thou, pale face, sad portrait of myself dressed in black? What wilt thou, wicked bird of passage? Is it a dream? Is it my own image that I see in the glass? Who art thou, ghost of my youth, pilgrim whom nothing could tire. Tell me why I find thee on the shadow everywhere I go. Who art thou solitary visitor, assiduous host of my pains? What hast thou done to be condemned to follow me through the world? Who art thou, who art thou, my brother who appears to me only on the days of sorrow?

THE VISION

Friend, my father is also thine. I am not a guardian angel, neither the evil genius of men. I do not know where are directed the steps which I love in this little world in which we are.

I am not God, neither devil, and thou hast called me by my name when thou calledst me brother. Where thou wilt go I will always follow till the last day in which I will go to sit on thy grave Heaven hath entrusted thy heart to me. When thou sufferest, come to me without uneasiness; I will come after thee on the road, but I cannot touch thy hand, friend; I am

THE SOLITUDE.

A. De Musset.

IV.

INFAMY.

TO REV. HARTLEY CARMICHAEL, (*Hamilton, Ontario.*)

Three families, hungry, naked, shelterless, twelve starved children, learning early in life how much pity exists in human hearts, wandering on every road, without finding shelter, stopped one day on that corner which once was called Switzerland the hospitable.

At the sight of them anger is suddenly shown. Rascals, vagabonds, beggars away with you! Let us cast this tiresome burden on our neighbors! Moneyless tourists, come, out of way! Off with you!! But our neighbors, thank God, have police like us for such visitors.

You may sometimes have seen panting sheep, ceaselessly worried by butchers' dogs with hungry jaws, bleating in despair, hurrying and pushing, finding no place to run to, to fly to, to escape this horrible torture, since on every side they are ready to bite them. And the butcher's boy gleefully chuckles and hounds them on, "Bite him, there's a little one for you." It is blood, it is flesh that the dog tears. It is an eye torn out that hangs on the jowl. It is a life in tatters; but close to the shambles it is quicker work; and one gets through his business all the sooner.

So the poor wretches cast out on the frontier, twenty times are roughly repulsed. Driven on and back, over marshes, down ravines, through forests, caught, let go, caught again, from twilight to dawn, from dawn to eve, they go on again. Oh, horror! in vain with tears and cries the little ones shew the tormentors their bleeding feet; in vain the rain drenches them, freezes them; no christian offers them a place under his roof; no hearth for a moment warms the pale and fleshless bodies of these wretched creatures.

Exhausted, they complain in a voice scarcely audible, "Mother, I am hungry, cold; mother my feet are bleeding; oh, mother, wait a little." But the orders are stern. Living or dead, they must leave the country without delay. They must tramp, still tramp; and the police have many other cares, besides these cries and tears.

Drag them, beat them, if their spirits break down. No doubt the rod will restore their strength. Let us see how orders are carried out, and if to excel in this noble competition the zeal of different districts is unequal, so that we may give the prize to the most brutal.

When there comes to us, dragging on a useless life, some worn-out millionaire, well taught the respect due to money, we sniff him and require nothing more; we pass him by as respectable, and humoring his whims, we find a virtue in his every vice.

Scruples and morality we keep for the poor. Let us be proud of our hospitality; it is like a tavern dog who humbly fawns on his master's customers, loves good clothes, hates tramps, and always bites rags and licks velvet.

Poverty, poverty, how bitter is thy wrath, and what a crushing burden is thy load of misery! Oh, mother of insults, what gall, what hatred, what fear, dost thou pour during thy long embraces, on those whom thou choosest, cleaving to them like a hideous leprosy, more deadly every day.

Never gaining a step, the poor man tramps day by day, wearing out his whole life in a fight with famine, to add to the cares of to-day more racking than yesterday's, those of to-morrow, which wake him at night; unless, indeed, he spend the night in ruining his eyes in order that another may be amused, or glitter for an hour or two; to see his dear ones hopelessly languish in want; to suffer in their suffering; to have less rest than the cattle; and yet to dread losing a thankless labour, and in order to keep it, to endure everything, contempt, hard words, from him who flings him a scrap of work.

That is his fate, and his mildest fate, too; that is what he is when he has food, when he is to be envied. Ah! now I understand knavery and cunning; the selling of soul and body to avoid such misery; every means being good to heap up money; for all is forgiven except the crime of an empty purse.

I feel myself shuddering with profound fear, for those who have bread, for the world's lucky men, when I see them teach the hideous lesson that there is no room in the sunshine except for them, that for them grow the flowers of this human life, for others the thorns and endless woe.

Ye rich! open your eyes, it is now or never! There are noble hearts among you, I know there are, and pride has always saved me from envy, but most of you have only seen one aspect of life, only the laughing side of this twofold world; ah! you would tremble to see the other!

Find a quick remedy for this gnawing evil. In prudence or in pity, come to help so many wretches whose groans becoming every moment more distinct, are changing into shrieks which, deaf though you be, the noise of your feasts cannot drown.

At least let fear loosen your fingers. Sometimes after ball or concert, you throw in this bottomless pit alms which men applaud, and which fall like a drop of water in a huge conflagration; then, fools, you think you have satisfied this hungry crowd who gnash their teeth.

Apportion, then your balm to the horror of the wound. The workman, aghast at the future, must have a labor less thankless, so that he may think of his children, of his old age, without turning pale; he must live and must have some joy, some little of the happiness which Heaven sends you.

Make haste to weep for every moment! Some day death will come, an unbidden guest, to sit at your banquet Then for the evil, which you have permitted, having been able to prevent it, on earth, you, oh, ye rich, shall answer for it tooth for tooth, eye for eye, body for body.

For him whom poverty drags into crime, for the maiden whom poverty defiles and throws into the street, for the cheat, the groveler, the covetous, for all those whom famine ruins, the anger of God, taking shape before your eyes, will ask of each of you, "Cain, what hast thou done with thy brother?"

In the name of earth and heaven help the poor. Keep a little money for his cup of wormwood. In your feasts, your balls, your games, let the memory rise that elsewhere some are desolate! Give, before it is taken away from you, for fear lest the flock who bleat to-day, may roar to morrow.

A. Richard.

V.

SAINT-SYLVESTER.

TO PROF. DANIEL WILSON, LL. D.
(*President of University College, Toronto.*)

The year is departing. When a mere boy, ignorant of life, these days to me were so beautiful, and such holidays. Gaily, with my soul full of hope, I ascended those hard steps built up with tombs.

The pride of being, and of growing, shone on my face; under my golden hair, I showed myself a fair flowering shrub of which the living sap drinks and overflows in the sunlight.

If I counted the days, it was not for complaining of the days, already past, which had fallen as dead branches; without fear I could contemplate the future, and without remorse I could enjoy the present.

Far, very far from the ancestral hearth with empty heart, mournful spirit and broken body, forsaken amidst the swarming city, sad, depressed, martyrized, to-day the future frigthens me.

To me it is like a dream, in which the pains of the day come back in turn to persecute us with human face, and, without rest, scourge us with love.

A. Richard.

VI.
THE TWO MOTHERS.

TO HON. CHRIS. S. PATTERSON.
(Judge of the Court of Appeal.)

> "I must go, and must take away from thy arms, oh, poor wretch, this my darling, who has made thee so happy."

I.

On the river Loire which, like a silver thread, runs over a hundred miles of happy land, proud and gay, the citadel of Saumur raises its head.

Like fresh beauties bathing themselves in the sea, her white houses extend along the river, half naked and half masked by vineyards and roses. Neither heat nor frost. It is an eternal spring. Oh, yes! beautiful and cheerful is the citadel of Saumur.

And there near the walls, like a soft pillow, is a gentle declivity with his mantle of verdure and the shadows of its avenues. But this verdure, and these flowers are not a complete paradise, and, mixed with such a celestial smile, is a house of sorrows.

Yes, a mad-house is at the extremity of the avenue. Amidst the silence of the night, amidst the gloomy wailing of the wind, are heard, interrupted, plaintive and deep sounds of lament, merry songs or strange voices, blasphemies and atrocious laughs.

And a strong feeling, of which nobody dares to ask the reason, forces every person to pay a visit to this living churchyard.

II.

On the last hour of a splendid sunset a beautiful young lady, giving her hand to her little daughter, ascends the hill. How charming was the little angel of five years, dressed in white, fresh, smiling, handsome and nimble.

The shining fair hair descends on her shoulders like waves, and, with her provoking looks, call for kisses. "Mother, can you tell me how those poor madmen live? Oh! how anxious I am to see them; mother, come."

The door is open, they ascend two stairs, they are in the asylum court. It was the time of the daily walk, the hour of the gaiety. One walks heavily, another recites, and another sings. Some jump up and down, some sit on the ground and others laugh.

A woman with loose hair and a dark petticoat, alone, far away in the corner, sits on a bench as if tired by long work. On her pale cheeks there is an old trace of tears. She turns around her stupid and dull glazed eyes.

God had given her as a token of a first love a girl whose face was as beautiful as that of a cherub. How she did love her dear daughter, how she watched her white cradle! Holy and deep affection! For this happy mother her girl was the world. A cruel illness had stolen this gem of her life, and heart-broken from the great sorrow she became mad, and for five years the poor wretch waited for her darling, and asked of all, if they had seen the lost one. Everybody who saw her with this intense pain engraved on her squalid forehead feels in his own soul a charm forcing him to tears. The kind lady approached near the unhappy mother, probably moved by such great sorrow.

Clinging to the skirt of her dress her little daughter thrusts forward her head, and with her eyes filled with tears, she said: "Poor thing!" Then softly approached the mad woman and with her little hand caressed her dark hair.

Shaken at this touch the unhappy one turns a look to the little angel, and a strange light shines in her eyes; then fixedly looking at her, she uttered a cry, opened her arms, and with an impetuosity of affection pressed the little one to his breast.

"Oh, my daughter, my dear daughter, how strong is this joy which overflows my heart! Almighty God, let me die in such happiness! Die? Who speaks of death? To live, I say, yes, I will live now that I have found thee and I will live always near my child.

"Come, sit here on my knees; let me kiss thy beautiful eyes, let me forget these few years of horrid anguish. From the very first day I lost thee, my eyes had no more tears, but the excessive ecstasy of this hour makes me weep anew.

"Tell me, where, where thou hast been all these years I was in search of thee? Hast thou perhaps been in the joy of the other life? But even in heaven in vain thou hast asked my sweet kisses, and now thou comest back to the loving embraces of thy mother. Thou comest now and wilt fly no more from these arms. I would rather die, Oh, yes, I feel that surely I would die, if again thou wert taken away from me."

III.

In such a way she spoke and convulsively pressed the girl to her panting bosom, and, in the intoxication of her deluded affection, kisses without number came from the burning lips. It was a fever of infinite love that sweetly melted her heart. The dear girl with her little hand caressed the dark hair, and, in return, kissed the unhappy woman and smiled at her with love's smile, the young mother not daring to trouble the joy of such a brief enchantment.

In the meantime the falling evening's twilight was shedding its pale light, and the dread band of guards opened the door of the inner staircase, the clock of the asylum calling the family of the lunatics to their respective cells. The kind stranger who feared to destroy the joy of this holy mistake approached near the poor mad woman, telling her in a pitiful voice of love, "I must go and I must take away from thy arms, poor wretch this my darling, who has made thee so happy!" Jumping up the mad woman with ferocious fear pressing the girl to her breast, "Who art thou," she cried to her with harsh voice, "who comest to trouble my motherly affection?"

"Knowest thou not that neither Satan nor God could ravish me of my little angel? Away, far from me. Woe to him who will dare to touch only a hem of her dress. Rather that permit her to be taken from my arms, I would rather she should die, oh, yes, I will kill her rather than lose her again."

Neither prayer nor threat could subdue the delusion of her mind, and with her lean arm raising the little girl, if anyone came forward, only a step, she meant to throw her on the ground, and such was the strong resolution gleaming from her gesture and from her accents, that it was thought better to leave her alone, and to await the events of the night.

Therefore all retired, and she with the girl ran into her cell, and there, in haste putting in order the bed, laid her child in it, and, arranging with care the folds of the rough sheets, joyfully sits at the bedside looking at her, smiling and kissing her.

Under the pressure of the hand which softly caresses

the girl, she shut her large eyes, and, yielding to weariness and sleep, fell into a sweet slumber, whilst the mad woman who was near her, soothed her repose with this song:

"Sleep, girl, my jealous eye as a guardian angel watches at thy pillow, and the interminable kiss like music soothes thy slumbers.

"Sleep, darling, and let me see thy moist brow, let me in the pure ecstasy of superhuman delirium intoxicate myself with thy warm breath.

"Beautiful thou art! thy cheek is rosy, thy head rests upon thy snow-white arm, and the halo of thy fair hair in a gentle disorder sorrounds thy forehead.

"Beautiful thou art! in the quiet rest of thy face I seem to see a ray of paradise, and in the celestial joy which shines in thy looks, I see the image of happy dreams.

"Dream, and in thy sleeping may the rainbow pour its colors, the stars their rays, the flowers their perfumes, and may the Holy Virgin* send from the paradise a company of angels to hover around thee."

IV.

There the voice become faint as the sound of a distant harp, and her tired forehead fell on the pillow of the little one. Once again the calm sleep of the happy days returned to her tired eyes.

The young mother absorbed in that fear which surpasses all fears, from the wicket of the iron door peeped into the dark room, where every movement, every kiss, every noise was a stroke of a poniard which pierced her heart.

But when all was silent, and there was only heard the cadence of two respirations, softly and gently a keeper crept into the room, advanced silently and without awakening the little one, who was sleeping, took her with him and shut the door.

The mother uttered a cry of joy, which echoed in the wide sonorous vaults, and kissing her dear lost angel, pressed her to her heart, and ran through the dark corridor with her tightly clasped in her motherly arms.

The mad woman awakened at the sound of the strange cry, perceived herself to be alone, looked around, and from the hole in the door, by the light of a dying lamp, she saw the white dress of the fugitive girl. A horrible cry of rage was heard, her eyes were suffused with blood, and with a foam on her livid lips she stretced forth her arms and rushed forward. Thrice she shook the unyielding door, then fell backwards a corpse.

Fusinato.

VII.

THE PROGRESS.

TO MRS. MILBURN, (*Buffalo*, N. Y.)

Vainly do we mingle arts and sciences, never, Oh! Nature, shall be able to reach thy magnificence so great and at the same time so simple. Always we shall be out-done by thy specimens, all our temples, all our palaces, all our immortal works are not comparable to the immense dome of the forests.

The most beautiful colors prepared by mankind become pale beside the pearly depth of four drops of water reflecting the pure sky. Color-changing mohair, fine laces, gauze, nor satin doth equal the wings of a beautiful butterfly fluttering into space.

The steamer which we see hurling itself on his fiery course, throwing into the air its thrilling voice, still nurtured the flames, and tamed by a gesture cannot follow the bird, whose towering flight, without breaking the harmonious silence, soars through the expanse of blue.

Then thousand torches of serene light which electricity, this new queen, has sent to human genius to fight with darkness, are these worth a single ray of the sun which glancing from a stream, gilds the branches; or the moon on a beautiful evening, or a glittering star?

All the bold dogmas, the dark systems invented at random by men, and which one sees dominating by turn here below, cannot equal that sublime belief in a God who must punish because He is just and holy, and Who at the same time well knows how to forgive because He is Love.

A. de Chambrier.

VIII.

THE STORM AT THE SAINT-BERNARD.

TO J. PESCIA M. D.,(*San Francisco, Cal.*)

> But it is done,—all words are idle.
> BYRON.

Come, little ones, do not cry! Soon you shall see your father. Thou the eldest say thy prayer! Come, children, do not cry.

"Mother, when will he return?"—"My son this time surely he has set off later. A business is discussed which ends at the table, and afterward one leaves it hardly able to see. At the table one has always something more to say."

"Mother it is dark"—"Child it is a cloud. The sky is bright at the village. Besides thy father is a prudent man; more than once he has made this journey. May Saint-Bernard make calm the wind."

Thus the mother, in her poor cottage, tries to hide the fear to which she is a prey: and many times, in cruel anxiety, stretches the ear, and thinking that somebody is walking, says to herself: why does he delay so long?"

Why does he delay so long? Look at the valley woman! Look at these whirlwinds and at the she-goat running towards thy solitary hut, and at the obscurity darkening the forests before the time.

Cross thyself, and listen to these creaking squalls whose doleful notes seem to speak of death: and to the fall far off which roars at intervals; and hear the voice of the torrents now swelling, now decreasing.

Dost thou not hear moaning the shivering leaves and the wind ingulfed in the deep woods, and the hurricane, carried on its powerful wings, plunging from the top of the mountains in the gloomy valley?

Poor woman!—In spite of so many signs of storm a peasant at the fall of the day, was marching over the fearful Saint-Bernard. In the vigor of the age, and in order to see sooner again his rustic abode, he has despised many wise advices. He had left Aosta; alas! and the imprudent had passed before the hospice without entering it.

Cheerful he was going on through the mountain. Sometimes sinking waist-deep in the snow, he was saying, so little was he frightened, "It is nothing!" and laughed in getting out of the snow, then without fear, courageous, as he was in the middle of the country, he, careless of the weather, lighted his pipe and whistled an old tune loved by his children.

May God keep you friend. May the propitious Virgin drive back the storm to the extremity of the horizon and avert thy foot from the precipice! But better, if thou wishest to see again thy house, without delaying a moment go, return to the hospice! There are the guardian angels of the travelers; at the risk of their own they will save thy life.

The air became brisk. The sky covered. The clouds before scattered which one had seen shine enflamed, now lie close, black and full of havoc, like batallions formed for an attack. The avalanche soon will hinder the road. Do not go, do not go!

Already the snow whirls around him. He hears sounds which usually render men pale, and that nameless voice which continually resounds, now seeming to cry, now to roar. It is the wind of the desert! It is the voice which in this place of woe nobody hears without trembling, which no other voice could resemble.

In the plain when the storm comes, the waters with their roars answers to its voice. The tree of which in its rage it tries to bend the head, stirs and stands erect hissing. In the mountains instead nothing answers to the storm, there nothing stops it. No rival roaring has ever moderated there the horrible majesty of this dreaded voice.

The unfortunate insists. He marches. At the end of an hour he begins to feel his leg dull. "Pshaw! it is the wind. Let us reach home! But I do not know why I am growing cold."

Wretch! What hast thou done? Who is able to preserve thee to thy wife who cries, to thy children? Do not hope for any help here below: God only can save thee.

He goes, goes. He feels the great allurement of a sleepiness which oppresses him and which he vainly tries to drive back. "I wish to sleep a while to acquire strength," says he, "in order to pursue my journey." Go, go on imprudent! Thou must endeavor not to yield to the spell which lulls thee to sleep. Go on. To sleep here, it is death.

He sits. His eyes soon close to the light. Confused but attractive objects deceive him. He believes he sees afar his hut, and hears walk his wife and his children. "Well," says he opening his eyelids "I must go. I see them. They come. I am better." Then he gets up, and falls, closing the eyes.

Later, in the savage little valley, a traveler, passing, met, at the edge of the road, a pale-faced mother, whose young children were tendering the hands for alms, saying, "God may help you in your journey!" He wished to know their story. "Our father died," they answered.

A. Richard.

IX.

THE UNKNOWN LIGHT.

To Miss Fanny Lee, (*Chicago*, Ill.)

When darkness comes, be the night cloudy or clear, suddenly on the distant heights I see shining a light which may be taken for a golden star. Every evening without fail it glistens at the hour when the hills are vanishing into the gloom, which slowly veils the world as it goes to rest.

Often I contemplate this solitary ray, which reaches me full of vague mysteries. Sometimes it seems to me that it lures me towards it, and a thousand strange desires thrill my being. I should like to turn aside from beaten tracks and direct my steps to this light which beams and gleams. I let my heart wander at my fancy's pleasure, and by turn a thousand visions pass before my eyes, soon to vanish.

First it is a young golden-tressed maiden, with large blue eyes filled with brightness so serene and pure that they make one dream of heaven.

Thoughtful and diligent she sews unceasingly; she wishes to finish her task this very evening, but often her sweet sparkling eyes turn towards the easy chair where her grandfather is slumbering, while the lamp sheds a reddish glow on the forehead of this noble white-haired old man.

Or it is a young shepherd who to rest himself from his weary labor comes to meet his betrothed and sits down beside her; he is strong and manly, she beautiful and active, and near both, a mastiff their faithful companion sleeps with his head resting on the ground.

In low tune they murmur sweet things to each other,

they expect to wed in the time of roses when birds make their nests, and—what peals of laughter! The dog pricks up his ears, and with his big, sleepy eyes half open watches them like an old and trusted friend.

Perhaps it is a learned man, a thinker, an artist, who seeks the calm, who is sad in the crowd, and who gives the watches of the night to toil. He thinks himself forgotten in his severe retreat, not guessing that my heart piercing earth's fogs, understands him, and that my eyes follow him.

Or again in the depths of my memory, stumbling over the remains of ancient history, I think of some gnome seated near a tomb where sleeps a princess with long raven black hair, her pale face strangely serene, waiting to be awakened by a young and beautiful prince.

Alas! And it is thus that I preserve my dreams! I remember them always without fatigue and without rest. More than once I have said to myself: "To-morrow at dawn I will go in person to search for the last word of this problem...." but the following day never finds me on the road.

I am afraid of seeing my palace of chimeras crumble; the sweet illusions of my heart are dear to me. I love so much to dream alone in the darkness. Seeing thee near, thou, modest lamp, surely I should say: "Alas! poor poet, thy dreams are better than reality!"

A. de Chambrier.

X.

MONOLOGUE

of

CHRISTOPHER COLUMBUS.

TO THE CONSUL OF ITALY, CAV. G. M. GIANNELLI.

I am dying, old and wretched, and it was right that I should die in such away! My life, toiled through suffering, ends with grief; but amidst all, God granted so great and infinite a joy, that every pain compared to it causes a smile. God, who, when He pours on the world a ray of eternal light, recommends it to Italy, His beautiful Italy thus spoke to me: "Daring Genoese, try the sun's path!"

And I turned my eyes to the West, and I saw a new world, as it were, rise from the waves; immense forests of unknown trees, immense rivers, immense plains. There were the softs fruits which distant India ripens, which Europe envies and desires; birds nameless with us, different wild beasts, seas filled with pearls, and mountains of gold—and the voice said: "Go; come back and tell the story."

But I am poor; sails do not spread at my command. I have nothing but a thought! And I brought my thought to the crowned heads of the world and asked a little gold for recompense. Alas! I was derided. For three long lustres I was scorned and went wandering about, and nobody understood me. I heard not, I saw not!

Here, bring me nearer to the balcony; for pity's sake do not take away from me the sight of the sea! The sea! the sea! my kingdom, the friend of my youth and of my glory! let me greet it a last time, and let me depart on that yourney from which nobody returns.

I was so glad, so serene when, for the first time, I challenged it. Courageous, I pushed myself on its open bosom where man's eye never yet reached. Foolish cowardice imagined it to be filled with monsters and terrors. I was not afraid.

Fly my ship; if my heart beats it is not for fear of the waves but of my followers. Fly, fly my ship, let not mischievous omens arrest thy swift course. A new land is there. Gaily and speedily let us make sail for the foreign shore; let us follow. God protects the bold undertaking. The wind is propitious, and the waves are gentle.

But already days go by, months have passed away, and no trace of new countries is perceived. Our life is always between heaven and sea, and confidence has disappeared from every face. What more can I do to encourage these men who only understand the vily sound of gold? I see other stars and other poles! " Three days more, and if our hopes are vain, I surrender myself to you."

Here we see flocks of birds rapidly fly from the West; sea-weeds and cleft from lands not distant. Land! land! A panting cry breaks the eternal silence of the sky. It is the land! it is the land! Who could now describe my joy? A light seen from afar in the dark air gives strength to the assured heart and to the tired hand. Forward! forward! Here is the dawn. Perhaps is my dream? No, no, this is the longed-for land, virgin, beautiful, dewy—beautiful like a bride given as a reward to valour, fair and flowery like the hope courted by me for so many years. See the sun advances; see the land smiles with proud life! Furls the sails. lower the boat. Oh, beloved land, at last I kiss thee.

The great work is accomplished! Am I not now the master of my land and of my sea? Where is my royal palace? Where are my councillors, my jewels, my crown? Ferdinand where is thy faith?

Thou wast sitting proud in the conquered Alhambra. Granada lay vanquished at thy feet. A wandering Italian, burdened by thought, whom anguish had made old before his time, leading by the hand a little boy, came to thy throne. Around it were princes, lords, captains, and all Spain's ancient splendor. What, powerful king, on that day said the unknown Genoese?

"Sire," said he, and he spoke without trembling, "fortune made thee sovereign of Aragon, love made thee master of Castille, war gave thee the beautiful kingdom of the Moors. Well I will do for thee more than fortune, love and war already have done, I will give thee a world."

And then Oh, king, when from the far ocean unexepected I returned and brought thee gold and jewels of thy new kingdom, thine without a drop of bloodshed, and to thy dumfounded sages and proud councillors haughtily I answered with facts, showing the proofs of the glorious achievement; what saidst thou, Oh king? "Genius is the sparkle of an eternal idea, and is superior to every crown. Grandees of Spain off with your hats!" Now, I am the same Columbus. In the gold, the distant springs of which I opened, Europe floats, and Spain is plunged up to the neck. Poor and forgotten, I beg my living, crust by crust, and the discoverer of a new world has not a roof, nor a house where he may die in peace.

Oh, do not tell my grand-children such an infamy! Oh, do not say that these arms even yet keep the marks of chains, and that, in the place of my triumph, I lived a prisoner! Cruel story! If it was fated that such a recompense should follow the benefit, God be thanked, that I have not done it for Italy.

It was right, it was right; see the beautiful country streaming with blood and with massacre. Of the people who butcher, and the people who suffer, which is the savage? Crime! crime! The sword is plunged into the breast of innocent brethren, but this was not my intention when I undertook to guide you, ye wicked! It is not gold that tempts wickedness, but vice is followed by useless offenses; these faithless men have made the Cross a pretext for butchery, the Cross, law of eternal pity.

Cease, ye cruel ones, what rage maddens you? Is gold not enough, that you wish even for blood? And cannot blood quench your horrible thirst? If this is valor what cowardice be? Shut out from my last moments this fatal scene! Let me not see these horrors. Already high vengeance is moved, is awakened—it roars—it falls—and first on me.

It was right! it was right! I bow my head. Oh sea! The sight of thee is remorse to me. Though innocent, we are accomplices to great disasters! The time will come when on blood and crime will rest the forgetfulness of centuries, and when from this new partnership will come to the universe as much good as formerly evil was produced, then amidst far posterity my name may be blessed, and a reward of honor more glorious, because longer delayed, may comfort my weary bones.

Now cover my face—I die in peace.

Gazzoletti.

XI.

THE PIRATE'S SONG.

TO A. NARDINI,(*San Francisco*, CAL.)

With ten guns on each side, the wind right aft, and all sails set, a brig does not plow the sea, but flies. The pirate vessel, for her bravery called the "Feared," well known in the water from one shore to the other.

The moon shines on the sea, amongst the sails sighs the wind, and by a slight movement raises waves of silver and blue. And the pirate captain, gaily singing on the poop beholds Asia on one side, Europe on the other and there before him Stamboul.

"Sail on my ship without fear, inasmuch as no unfriendly sail, nor storm, nor calm is able to overtake thy stern or to conquer thy valor. In spite of the English I have taken twenty prizes and a hundred nations have lowered their flags at my feet.

"That my ship is my treasure, liberty my God, the force and the winds are my laws, and the sea my only fatherland.

"Let blind kings move fiery wars between themselves for the sake of a span of land, whilst here I have for mine, all that is grasped by the wide sea to whom nobody has dictated laws. And now, there is no shore, wherever it be, nor a flag of renown which has not felt my right hand and proclaimed my bravery,

"That my ship is my treasure, etc.

"At the cry of 'Sail, oh!' it is something to see how it turns and takes measures to avoid every snare, inasmuch I am the king of the sea, and my anger is to be feared. In the prizes, I divide the booty equally, keeping for myself only a wealth, beauty without rivals.

"That my ship is my treasure, etc.

"I am sentenced to death; I laugh at it. Let fortune not forsake me and regarding the one who condemns me, perhaps I shall hang him to the yard-arm of his own ship. And if I fall? What is life I gave it up the same day, when, like a brave man, I threw away from me the yoke of a slave.

"That my ship is my treasure, etc.

"My best music is the northern wind, the trembling and noise of grating cables, the roar of the blackened sea and the thunder of my guns, and amid the violent din of the thunderbolts, mid the howling wind, I sleep calm, lulled by the sea."

Don Jose de Espronceda.

XII.

CHARITY.

TO REV. D. J. MACDONELL.

When the pining flower that summer causes to fade leans toward the burning soil to die, and to quench the fire by which it is devoured, asks and begs only a drop of water; without rain or dew this dying complaint falls with the wind's breath.

So when the unhappy being drags himself along, bent from the cradle under troubles, oppressed by his burden, if the arm of his brother does not support his misery, if some sweet voice does not speak a word which raises and comforts him, he must fall under its weight.

Oh, sublime charity, balm of grief, thou whose sight inspires courage, thou who driest tears; beloved daughter of God! Pain and bitter complaint are silent before thee; peace is in thy mouth, and those touched by thy hand suddenly lose their fears.

He who lost in doubt and in despair has long ago strayed from the right path, by thee is brought repentant to God whom he had forgotten, and thou restorest hope in him who hope no more.

Oh, Supreme Majesty, thy sovereign order has said: "Love thy neigbor as thyself." The man only to whom misery never is troublesome is just in thine eyes. If in heart he is poor, by the good actions he has done, he will become rich in heaven.

A. Richard.

XIII.

WHY LOVEST THOU ME?

TO C. BARSOTTI, M. D.

I.

Why lovest thou me young girl? Dost thou know who I am? A young poet who always runs in the same road amongst thorns and flowers, and never arrives at the goal. The poor poet is a butterfly, and, like this one, loves the pictured flower beds, and now rising up, then down, plays with the breeze and search the sun and the flowers.

The little butterfly is happy with a few drops and with a little fragrance; a drop of dew quenches its thirst, a rose leaf is its room.

Often foreign to what it hears or sees, it is pleased with its golden wings and flowers, contented with the virtue God gave it, thus passing its life in peace.

The lion passes, the king of the forest, and seeing it going from flower to flower, "This is the happiest one," says he, "that flying, passes the time in making love."

The fox passes, busy with its cunning, and scoffs at the sincere butterfly, which without any snare or any offence, goes flying alone, always alone.

The magpie passes, deafening the valley, the magpie always slanderous and brating. The screech-owl passes, found of ruins, enemy of love and peace.

But the butterfly, which is born for other purposes, passing, does not look at them, and does not care for them, and always flies, and it is always in love, such as nature made it.

II.

With a few drops, with few perfumes, the poor poet also nourishes himself. Amongst the flowers of his hopes, he too is a happy and nimble butterfly.

He opens the little window at the first dawn, and singing, he salutes the rising sun. The breeze repeats his verses of love and the heart of any who listen to him trembles.

Near the setting of the sun he moans and cries, and he recites the verses thou singest; they are the songs of his mountains, those songs which he never forgets.

The note of that sweet song trembles as the flower of the land which gave him birth. There is the word, there is the laugh, the weep, there are the eyes and the lips of his girl.

III.

Like prophetic birds his verses go from sea to sea, from land to land. Different people repeat them in the time of peace and war.

The poet is poor, and every one says so; but he has a heart as great and as deep as the sea, and to look at him he seems the happiest and the richest man in this world.

So very poor, and so very rich, he passes among the people humble and proud, and through his fatal journey he tires the light of free thought.

And he who meets him looks at him and greets him with the most beautiful name that resounds in the world, and that name which the world gives him is the prettiest ornament of his wreath.

Glances, smiles and courteous receptions are not denied to him, and he smiles to all; but believe me, my Lina, these are his only joy, these his only fruits. And these fruits will not be envied by the animals, of shrewd and doubtful faith, screech-owls, foxes and lions, because they know, too well they know, that the little butterfly, does not desire anything else.

IV.

Yes, I too, oh! Lina, am like the butterfly, I that in every road am searching for flowers: my amorous soul runs after that desire which drags it.

It runs from morning to evening, and itself, poor thing, does not know why it runs, and the more it pricks itself the more approaches to those roses which desire colors. And believes to suck in the lap of all the flowers drops of ambrosia to sweeten the song; but often, my Lina, those sweet humors are only drops of his own weeping.

Yes, butterfly I am, my Lina, and the native clod is generous of a hundred flowers; but these are perfumes, and the wind wafts them, the favors of my native land.

V.

Now thou knowest who I am, and I do not understand how thou, my girl, lovest me so much. Is it my poor name that is dear to thee, or perhaps is my plaintive song? But name and song shall pass; my poor verses are flowers, and thou well knowest it, that the sweetest odor of the prettiest flower does not live longer than a day.

And then dost thou not see how much harmony of life and love there is around us? Dost thou not see how in the same day this universe almost is born and dies?

And perhaps there where now life dances, death shall raise her black tents, and the people of free hope may be a heap of bones and bands.

And those roses, where now the nightingales warble perhaps shall be turned into sprigs and amongst them there shall only be heard the sharp hissing of savage snakes.

And perhaps here where I am singing of affection, and where so many others also will sing, this thy little blessed village, which completely enraptures me with its beauties, shall be changed into wood, and every thicket will give a volume of doubtful stories, and the crow's song shall be heard, the old sybil of the desert.

VI.

All falls and rises again, and everybody perceives this, but love, love, Lina, does not die; his seat is in our soul. Everlasting as the soul is love.

And thy love shall never change its intensity; that is what I only wish from thee. Of love, only of love, speak always to me, inasmuch as he who speaks of love speaks of God.

With the elegance of a nod and a smile, thou awakest in me sweet and new poetry. Through thy pretty blue eyes, truly it seems to me, I see Paradise.

G. A. Costanzo.

XIV.

POOR BARD!

TO L. STECCHETTI.

> As a child in thy presence I lowered my eyes, I cowered at thy knees as fawningly as a whipped spaniel. With my proud forehead bent I kissed the hem of thy garment. I suffered, I cursed, I cried and thou laughedest.
>
> Now I rise from my cowardly baseness, and break my chains, I feel ashamed of me and my love, I rise, and I despise thee.
>
> STECCHETTI, (Anger.)

Poor poet! in what proud remorse of past cowardice consumest thou thyself? Thou risest and insultest, and I hardly say, if thou wert more coward then, or less proud now. Thou risest and insultest. Ah! do not repeat the insult which so imprudently came out from thy heart! This is not pride, it is not courage, it is not freedom.... on my word it is love!

Behold with what pain and blind rage thou throwest mud on the once worshipped idol! How bleeds the heart which is cursing! Cease thy scoffing. Woe if she hear the sound of thy scoffs, woe if she sees thee! To-morrow on going again to kiss her foot, perhaps thou shall pay dear for her forgiveness.

If thou art a poet do not insult the sacred flame which lightened thy heart if it dictated to thy dust a single poem and gave a single spark to thy grief.

Do not insult her, do not cry out that the desire for

"vile mud" enflamed thee. Wretched one, how shalt thou say to the world "of that mud I had made a God."

Ah! do not speak of this dream which is fixed in thy heart, Oh, do not soil that shadow. In order to possess that right thou oughtest have never placed her on the altar.

Until from thine eye and from thy suffering spirit shall come but a single tear, respect the dream which opened an heaven for thee, respect the mud which inspired thee with a song.

If truly thou art now strong and free, if thy insults are born from a redeemed heart, I offer thee another trial. Go to her, gaze on her face, without moving an eye.

Defy the old power of her eyes without experiencing a chill in thy veins. Look at her face without desire or anger, without scorn or hope. And try to breathe without shock in the wake of her hidden perfumes. Approach her, touch one of her hands without feeling a shudder in thy bones.

And when the heart shall no more give thee a shudder, a tear or an oath, poor poet, oh, then, only then, thou canst boast of having conquered love.

No! this roar of rage is not the comfort thou are searching for. Poor poet! Thou shalt not be cured except on the day thou shalt forgive.

F. Cavallotti.

XV

HOPE IN GOD.

TO J. DUNFIELD, M. D.(*Canada.*)

As long as my feeble heart, yet full of youth, shall not have bid farewell to his last illusions, I would abide by the old wisdom which has made a demi-god of the sober Epicurus. I would live, love, accustom myself to my equals, go in search of joy without relying upon it, do what has been done, be what I am, and carelessly lift my eyes to heaven.

It is impossible. Infinity torments me. In spite of myself I cannot think of it without fear or hope, and notwithstanding all what has been said, my reason is frightened at seeing it, and not being capable of understanding it. What is this world? and what we come to do in it, if to live in peace, it is necessary to veil heaven? To pass like sheep with our eyes fixed on the ground and to forsake all else, can that be called happiness? No, it is to cease to be a man, and degrades the soul. Chance has put me in the world. Happy or unhappy, I am born of a woman, and I cannot throw of humanity.

What can I do then? "Be merry," says paganism, "be merry and die." "Hope" answers Christianity, heaven always watches, and thou canst not die."

Between these two roads I hesitate. I would wish to follow a more easy path, but a secret voice tells me that with regard to heaven one must believe or deny. This is my opinion too. Tortured souls cast themselves, sometimes into one, sometimes into the other, of these two extremes. The indifferent are atheists,—if they would doubt only for a day, they could not sleep. I yield, and as the matter leaves in my heart a desire full of dread, I will bend my knees, I wish to believe and to hope.

Here I am in the hands of a God more dreadful than all evils of this world put together. Here I am alone a wandering, weak and miserable creature beneath the eye of a witness who leaves me not. He watches me, he follows me. If my heart beats too quick I offend his dignity and his divinity. A precipice is opened under my steps. If I fall into it to expiate an hour, an eternity is needed. My judge is a tyrant who deceives his victim. For me everything becomes a snare and changes its name. Love becomes a sin, happiness a crime, and all the world is for me a continuous temptation. I have nothing more of humanity about me. I await the recompense, I try to avoid the punishment; fear is my guide, and death is my only aim.

Nevertheless, it is said that an infinite joy will be the share of some elect. Who are those happy beings? If thou hast deceived me, wilt thou again give me life? If thou hast told me the truth, wilt thou open the heavens?

Alas! this beautiful country, promised by thy prophets, if it really exists, must be a desert. Thou requirest those choosen ones to be too pure, and when this happiness arrives they already have suffered too much. I am a man, and I will not be less, nor attempt more. Where should I stop? If I cannot believe in the priest's promises shall I consult those who are indifferent?

If my heart, wearied by the dream which troubles it, returns again to reality for consolation, at the bottom of the vain pleasures called into my aid I find a disgust that kills me. In the same day in which my thoughts are impious, in which to end my doubts I wish to deny, even though I possessed all that a man could desire, power health, wealth, love, the only blessing of this world, though the fair Astartè worshipped by Greece should come from the azure islands, and should open her arms, though I could come into possession of the secret of the earth's fertility, and thus changing at my fancy living matter, create a beauty for myself alone, though Horace, Lucretius and old Epicurus seated near me, should call me happy, and those great lovers of nature should sing the praises of pleasures, and the contempt of the gods, I would say to all, "In spite of our efforts I suffer, it is too late, the world has become old, an infinite hope has crossed the earth, and against our will, we must raise our eyes to heaven."

What else remains to me to try. Vainly my reason tries to believe, and my heart to doubt. The christian affrights me, and in spite of my senses I cannot listen to what the atheist says to me. True religious people will call me an impious, the indifferent will call me a fool. To whom shall I address myself, and what friendly voice will comfort my heart wounded by doubt?

It is said that there exists a philosophy which can explain everything without revelation. Granted. Where are those makers of systems who, without faith know how to find the truth? Weak sophists, who believe only in themselves, what are their arguments, what their authorities? One shows me, here below, two principles at war, which alternatively conquered, are both everlasting.(1) Another, far away in the desert heaven discovers a useless God Who will have no altar.(2) I see Plato dreaming, and Aristotle thinking. I hear them, I praise them, but I pursue my way. Under absolute kings I find a despot God, now they spoke to us of a republican God; Pythagoras and Leibnitz transfigure my being. Descartes leaves me perplexed. Montaigne, after great examination cannot understand himself. Pascal trembling tries to escape his

---

(1) Manicheans.   (2) Theism.

own visions. Pyrro blinds me and Zeno makes me insensible. Voltaire throws down all he sees standing. Spinosa tired of trying the impossible, vainly searching for his God, ends by seeing him everywhere. With the English sophist, (1) man is a machine, finally, out of the fogs comes a German rhetorician, (2) who, finishing the ruin of philosophy, declares Heaven empty and proves that there is nothing.

Here are the wrecks of human science! and after five thousand years continually doubting, after such a great and persevering work, behold there the last result at which we have arrived. Poor, foolish, miserable brains, who have explained all in such different ways, to reach Heaven you need wings. You had the desire, but faith was not with you. I pity you; your pride came from a wounded soul; you have felt the pangs of which my heart is filled, and you well knew this bitter thought which makes man tremble whenever he considers infinity. Well come on, let us pray together, let us abjure the misery of our childish calculations, of such vain work. Now that your bodies are dust I will pray for you on your graves. Come pagan rhetoricians, masters of sciences, christians of old times, and thinkers of the present age, believe me, prayer is a cry of hope. Let us ourselves address to God. He is good, without doubt, He forgives you. All you have suffered is forgotten. If Heaven is a desert, we shall offend nobody, if there is One Who hears us, may He pity us.

PRAYER.

Oh, Thou, Whom nobody has been able to know, and whom none has denied without lying, answer us. Thou Who hast made me, and to-morrow shalt make me die.

---
(1) Locke.   (2) Kant.

Since Thou lettest us to understand thee, why, makest thou people doubt thee? What sad pleasure canst thou feel in tempting our good faith? As soon as a man raises his head he thinks that he sees thee in heaven: the creation, his conquest, in his eyes is only a vast temple. As soon as he descends into his inward he finds Thee. Thou livest in him. If he suffers, weeps or loves, it is his God Who has so willed. The noblest intelligence, the most sublime ambition is to prove Thy existence and in teaching Thy name. Whatever is the name given Thee, Brahma, Jupiter, Jesus, True Eternal Justice, all arms are extended to Thee. The last of the sons of the earth thanks thee from his heart as soon as to his misery is mixed a simple appearance of happiness. All the world glorifies Thee; the bird from his nest sings to Thee; and thousands of beings have blessed Thee for a drop of rain. Nothing has been done by Thee that is not admired; none of thy gifts is lost to us; and Thou cannot smilest without we fall on our knees before Thee. Why then Supreme Master, hast thou created evil so great that reason and even virtue tremble at its sight? Whilst so many things in the world proclaim the divinity, and seem to be witnesses of the love, power and kindness of a father; how is it that under the holy sky are seen actions so shocking as to check the prayer on the lips of the unhappy? How is it that in Thy divine handiwork are so many elements not in harmony? To what good are pestilence and crime? Just God, why death? Thy pity must have been great when with all its good and evil this marvelous and beautiful world, crying, emerged from Chaos! Since Thou wouldst submit it to the pains of which is replenished Thou oughtest not to have permitted it to discern Thee. Why lettest Thou our misery see and guess at a God? Doubt has brought desolation on the earth. We see too much or too little. If Thy creature is unworthy to approach Thee, Thou oughtest let nature veil and hide Thee. Thy power would have been left to Thee, and we chould have felt its blows; but quiet and ignorance would have lessened our griefs.

If our afflictions and pains reach not to Thy majesty, keep Thy solitary grandeur, shut forever Thy immensity; but if our mortal griefs can reach to Thee, and from the eternal plains, Thou hearest our sighs, break the deep vaults which covers creation, lift this world's veil, and show thyself a just and good God. Thou wilt see all over this earth an ardent love of faith, and the whole mankind will fall down before Thee. The tears which flow from men's eyes as a light dew will disappear in heaven. Thou shalt hear only Thy praises, and a concert of joy and love like that with which the Angels gladden Thy everlasting kingdom, and in this supreme HOSANNA, Thou shalt see at the sound of our songs, doubt and blasphemy fly away, whilst death itself will join its last accents to them.

A. de Musset.

XVI.

THE COAT.

TO ANGELO NICCOLAI, (*Lucca.*)

Thou reproachest me, Francis, and thou sayest that I forget my old friends. If, as before, poetry gives sweet food to thy beautiful soul, read MY COAT, and see if I can forget you, when I keep remembrance even of a very old worn-out coat. No, while a drop of blood runs in my veins, I would that we remain, " two souls with a single thought, two hearts beating in one."

TO MY COAT.

JOKE.

My poor coat, my sweet friend, it is true, thou art ragged, it is true, thou art old, but in happy as in hard times I had thee, an inseparable companion, and, remembering thee I love thee, nor I cast thee from me.

Let those who, fond of change, follow the fashion and let them admire my constancy. By experience, I have learned that, in this century, dress is everything.

Look at that nobleman, who upon his coat wears sewn a silk ribbon? If thou take off the dress, who, by his manners would honor him as a knight? Where are his grace and amiability? Where is the old time elegant bearing? Formerly it was the usage to protect oppressed ladies, now one strikes even his own wife.

Another is angry and raises row if people do not call him doctor. But could he be known as such without his gown? The ignoble crowd, wouldst thou believe? humbles itself, bends, to whom?—to a robe. Like the donkey, who was carrying the beautous image of Cytherea, while the frightened beast was passing, the people filled with devotion used to bow.

Oh, my very dear coat, never did I wear thee out of vanity, nor ever for debts wast thou pulled off, for even thou art ragged, I have paid for thee, with the honest fruit of my sweat, inasmuch as a noble soul is unused to sell an object of affection, but he has not the usual luck to find some one who pays clothes for him.

Under the sleeves one may see the threads, but that recalls me my glory, because I wore it when I, under the influence of poetical fire, was writing the *Naso* for you, my ladies.

Look, the collar, is already worn out on account of my turning here and there, and yet, it brings me no grief nor pain, but it is my tender keepsake, because I do remember those joyous days in which I felt in love with a young girl.

Often when sitting between mother and daughter, for the sake of propriety, using the most deep and subtle policy, I was convening now with the one, now with the other. But when speaking to the young one low in her ear, the cunning old lady would say, "What' that?" (with her elbow nudging mine,) and I would answer, "Oh, nothing" and address myself to the girl, that everlasting turning of my head was for my collar a great misfortune, and yet it does not grieve or pain me, it is the tenderest of my recollections.

When I am sitting near to ladies, I cannot act like a statue, I am ARETINO! I like to speak, and I like to look, and I like to move as much as I choose, and, if my collar must suffer on account of it, cannot be helped, the collar will have to be renowned.

Here where the coat meets near the stomach a button is missing. Of ten which were, now there remained nine,

ALICE DE CHAMBRIER

your number, daughters of Jupiter. Wanting some money, often I put my hands into the pockets, but in vain and yet that *deficit* does not grieve me, but all the more awakens the old **vein**, so that in my mind, I change my pamphlets into **money**.

Oh, how delightful to be a poet! All subscribe for friendship and all pay, how delightful! Then my ragged old **coat**, my ever faithful companion and friend, who with me wast in great Rome, and with me when I was admitted to the degree of doctor, (so that leaving thee, I should fear to lose half of **my knowledge**), thou art the sweet and only cause of my most happy days. Life on account of thee is to me dear and gay, since I learned to know mankind.

When thou wert renowned for fashionable style, amidst a vain and gallant world, and hadst the merit of being handsome, everybody took off his hat to me. In the vestibules wherever I went I used to hear repeated "Come in, come in." Great noblemen convened with me and servants called me *very illustrious*. I lived dear to the ladies, but, alas! Honor, kindness, all were addressed to thee! and now that thou no more excitest easy pleasure on account of thy shabby shapelessness, at balls, at clubs, I hear said: "With that coat you cannot pass," and if I go to visit any one, he sends words: "Nobody at home." Everybody avoids me, some shrewd ones, fear that I am going to ask a loan wherewith to have another made. My poor coat thou well seest that honors and kindnesses were addressed to thee. Yet to live with thee is dear and joyful to me, because I learned to know mankind.

Perish useless luxury, nor let me hear any more fashion praised by fanatics, fatal source of laziness and vexation. True happiness lurks amid shabby clothes.

Guadagnoli.

XVII.

THE JEANNETTE'S VICTIMS.

TO JOAN STOCKTON HOUGH, M. D.

The other day, in opening a newspaper, my eyes by chance fell on the following words: "THE JEANNETTE." The Jeannette! and, for a long time, I remained thoughtfully gazing into the space, and sad at heart.

My mind, carried far away, with a hasty ramble, had already rejoined those men, those sailors lost, feeble, tottering in the snow amidst the floating ice-bergs.

These records daily written by your hands at the time you saw all hope of help lost, when knowing perfectly that safety was impossible, you were obliged to look upon your best friends struck down by death, and withdraw from you, after having consoled them with a last ray of love and prayer.

You have not expressed in these records all that you suffered. Yet neither pain nor the infinite dread of such daily sad agony could conquer your courage or shake your faith, brave and valiant souls. Honor to you! Honor forever!

Thus all of them yesterday were unknown, but to-day are famous; they remained great at that dismal hour, and when my heart searches for them in their quiet rest, if they appear to me, it is only with the forehead encircled by the martyr's wreath.

Oh, you saw them drawing near to merciless death, and yet you have kept an ineffable hope. Grand it was to have remained alone in such a horrid place far from their home, from their country, without help and to have believed in God without murmuring and without complaining.

Oh, how great were they! strugglers! heroes! martyrs! Let us love the priceless offerings of these victims who sacrificed themselves to thy divine cause, LIGHT AND PROGRESS.

A. de Chambrier.

XVIII.

DANTE.

TO THE HON. JOHN BEVERLEY ROBINSON.

> La colpa seguirà la parte offensa,
> In grida come suol.
>
> DANTE.

It was evening. Deprived of its magnificence, the sun now arrived at the dimmed horizon, was departing silently, without strength, like an exiled king, who passes away unknown. Upright upon a hill whence Florence could be seen, leaning on his sword still unsheathed and bloody, a soldier, fierce in face, yet dusty from the battle scarcely ended, all of whose companions were flying at random, stood, casting on the distant city, a long and painful look. A deep sigh heaved his breast, his eye sparkled, and his voice made the hill tremble.

"Vanquished! exiled like a brigand! driven away by the fate of the battlefield! without even having the fortune to die fighting beneath our walls! Vanquished! From valley to valley to drag along my sad life, begging from half-hearted friends!—to eat the hard bread of alms until my last hour comes! these are the rights I have won!

"I must fly, then, far from thee, dear and ungrateful city—live and suffer far from thee without hope! Of all the misfortunes which from this moment will weigh on me, the greatest will be never to see thee again! Thou sun, who art dying continue thy course and illumine still the roof of my ancestors, and the holy place where under the black stone are sleeping in peace my mother and my father. Oh, why could I not sleep near them! Thou, beloved Beatrice, who scarcely hast touched our world while directing thy course toward heaven, in thy great glory dost thou still remember thy friend? Vision so short and so beautiful! Oh, bright day, what was thy to-morrow? Watch over me, radiant, immortal one! Sweet-eyed angel, cover me with thy wings! Happy star, point me out my way!"

Dante was silent, and as in the tempest the oak lowers the pride of its branches, the exile bent under the burden of his misfortunes, lowered his face, and, with tormented soul and eyes full of tears, tasted long the bitterness of his pains. A noise came to draw him from his thoughts, a noise feeble at first, but continually increasing, a terrible mixture of saddened bells, of a nation's curse, of songs of victors, and of cries of the vanquished.

This noise was the uproar of the people of Florence. Humbled on account of their fears, to feast their victory, they asked for vengeance, and without pity dragged to the scaffold many prisoners spared by the sword in battle.

Like a lion awakened by a sudden noise, which with flashing eyes rises and pricks up his ears, the soldier started at the words which reached him with the echo, and coming out from his sad repose for a moment listened to the brutal orgies; and then, with his arms extended toward his native city, thus addressed her:

"Senseless populace! Go on, ye who curse the sacrificed, and only help the strongest! Join death to thy pleasure. Mingle blood with the wine of thy feast. Laugh at the execution prepared for those who, moved by faith, have risked their life for thee!

Go on with thy work, and make haste. Canst thou in thy wisdom, know how many hours are needed to change joy into dread, and grief into joy,—how long last so sweet a power,—and if the oppressed remain long on their knees?

"Without doubt, puffed up by their good fortune, triumphant and full of bitterness, the *Neri* already say 'Our reign is sure!' Thinking this reign an easy task, and the league of the *Bianchi* crushed, they strike our remnants, and scoff at us with jest and sarcasm.

"Oh, *Neri*, know how to maintain yourselves kings of the present. I have the future, and you, I dare to think, will follow me thither. Ungrateful history may leave in darkness your great exploits. I, in this terrified world, just towards so great a glory, will immortalize you.

"Pouring infernal light on your venal spirits, I will, portray you to future ages, and will discover the niggardliness, the jealousy, the treachery, the hypocrisy of your hearts, and upon your soiled names will throw torrents of terrible verses. Oh, inconstant and deceitful people! I feel the day of vengeance coming! Tremble! I am the supreme wrath, bend thyself under its course, and may misfortune break thy pride; every hour will bring a new pain, and thou shalt torture thyself as a man alive in a tomb."

The night had come. A blast of tempest roared passing through the air; the dark heaven was reddening, the arm of the sad prophet seemed to threaten the perverse, and the inspired forehead of the divine poet was sorrounded by lightning.

From nation to nation, from place to place, untamed, uneasy, full of hatred and love, the great outlaw wandered twenty years, far from his birth-place, always dreaming of his return.

Until the last hour he cherished the hope of seeing this happy day. Death only took pity on his long sufferings; and the old Ghibelin never more saw Florence,—which has not even his remains within her walls.

A. Richard.

XIX.

PHANTOMS.

TO WM. OLDRIGHT, M. A., M. D.

I.

How many beautiful maidens have I seen die! It is destiny. A prey is necessary to death. As the grass must fall under the scythe, so, in the ball, the quadrille must tramp rosy youth under its steps. The fountain by irrigating the valleys must diminish its waters. The lightning must shine, but only for a moment. Envious April with its frosts must blight the apple tree, too proud of its odoriferous flowers, white as the snow of the spring. Yes, such is life. The darkness of the night follows the daylight, and to all will come the eternal awaking in heaven, or the abyss. A covetous crowd sits at the great banquet, but many of the guests leave their places empty and depart before the end.

II.

How many have I seen die! One was fair and blooming. Another seemed enraptured in a celestial music. Another with her arms uphold her bended head—and as the bird, which in taking flight, breaks the branch on which it rests—her soul had broken her body.

One pale, lost, oppressed by sad delirium, pronounced in a low voice a name forgotten by all, another dies away as a sound of a lyre, and another, expiring has on her lips the sweet smile of a young angel, returning to heaven. All frail flowers—dead as soon as born—halcyons drowned with their floating nests; doves sent from heaven to earth, who, crowned with grace, youth and love, numbered their years by the springs.

Dead! What? Already lying under the cold stone! So many charming beings deprived of voice and life! So many lights extinguished! So many flowers faded away! Oh, let me trample the dried leaves and lose myself in the depth of the woods.

Lovely phantoms! It is there in the woods, when in the dark I am thinking, it is there that by turn they come to listen and to speak to me. The twilight at the same time, shows and veils their number, but across the branches I perceive their glittering eyes.

My soul is a true sister to these beautiful shadows. For me and for them life and death have no laws—sometimes I help their steps—sometimes I take their wings. Ineffable vision in which I am dead and they alive like me. They lend their forms to my thoughts. I see, oh, yes I see them. They beckon me to come, and then, hand in hand, they dance around a grave, and, by degree disappearing softly, draw away, and then after I think and I remember.

III.

One especially—an angel—a young Spanish girl! White hands, her breast swelled by innocent sighs. Black eyes in which shone the looks of a Creole; and that indefinite charm, that fresh halo, which generally crowns a head of fifteen.

She died not for love. No, love had not yet brought her joy nor sorrow; nothing yet had made her rebel heart beat, and, when everyone, in looking at her, could not repress the words, " How beautiful she is!" none had yet uttered secretly the word of love. Poor girl! She loved dance too much—it was that which killed her. The charming ball! The ball full of delight! Her ashes still tremble with a gentle movement, if, by chance, in a fair night a white cloud dances around the crescent of the sky.

She loved dance too much! At the approach of a festival—three days before, she was continually thinking and dreaming of it—and for three nights ladies, music, dancers never tired, troubled her mind in her sleep, and laughed, and shouted at her pillows.

Jewels, necklaces, silk girdles of waving reflections, tissues lighter than bee's wings, festoons and ribbons to buy a palace, all those things occupied her fancy.

Once the festival begun—full of gladness she comes with her joyful sisters, furling and unfurling the fan in her fingers,—then sits amongst the silk dresses, and her heart bursts into glad strains with the many-voiced orchestra. What a true delight was it to look at her when she was dancing! Her garment tossed its blue spangles; her great dark eyes sparkled under the black mantle like a pair of stars under a dark cloud. She was all dance and laughter and mad joy. Child!

We admire her in our sad leisure moments, sad, because never at the ball our hearts were open, and in these balls, as the dust flies on the silk dress, weariness is mixed with pleasure. She, instead, carried by the waltzes or the polkas, was going up and down, hardly breathing, exciting herself with the sound of the renowned flute, with the flowers, with the golden candlesticks, with the attractive feast, with the music of the voices, with the noise of the steps.

What happiness for her to move, lost in the crowd, to feel her own senses multiply in the dance, so as not to be able to know is she were being conveyed by a cloud, or flying leaving the earth, or treading upon a waving sea.

At the approach of the dawn, she was obliged to depart, and to wait on the treshold till the silken mantle was thrown over her shoulders. Only then, this innocent dancer, chilled, felt the morning breeze play over her bare neck.

Sad morrow those following a ball! Farewell dances and dresses, and child-like laughter. In her, the obstinate cough succeeded the songs; the fever with its hectic color followed the rosy and lively delights, and the bright eyes were changed into lack lustre eyes.

IV.

She is dead! Fifteen years old, beautiful, happy, adored! Dead coming out from a ball which immersed all of us in mourning, dead, alas! And death, with chilly hands wrested her yet dressed from the arms of a mother mad with anguish, to lay her to sleep in the grave.

To dance at other balls she was ready, death was in haste to take possession of such a beautiful body, and the same ephemeral roses which had crowned her head and which blossomed yesterday at a feast faded in a tomb.

V.

The unhappy mother, ignorant of her fate, had placed so deep love on this frail stalk; to have watched her suffering babyhood so long, and to have wasted so many nights in lulling her when she cried, a tiny baby in her cradle. To what purpose? Now the girl sleeps under the coffin lid and, if in the grave where we have left her, some beautiful winter's night a festival of the dead should awaken her cold corpse, a ghost, with dreadful smile, instead of his mother, will preside at her toilette, and will tell her, "Now is the time," and with a kiss freezing her blue lips, will pass through her hair the knotted fingers, of his skeleton hand, and will lead her trembling to the ethereal chorus, flitting in darkness, and, at the same time on the gray horizon the moon will shine pale and full and the rainbow of the night will color, with an opal reflection, the silver clouds.

VI.

Young maidens who are invited by the gay ball, with its seductive pleasures, think of this Spanish girl. She was gay, and with a merry hand was gathering the roses of life, pleasure, youth and love! Poor girl! Hurried from feast to feast she was sorting the colors of this beautiful nosegay. How soon all vanished! Like Ophelia, carried away by the river, she died gathering flowers.

V. Hugo.

XX.

DAVID.

TO MISS SUSIE. E. WITHFORD, (CHICAGO, ILL.)

To contend with the giant Goliath, David had only his sling, but at the bottom of his boyish heart he had also a strong faith. He was perfectly aware that in order to save Israel, God would figth for him.

Calm and easy in mind, he set forth against the powerful Philistine who, with haughty and insolent look, smiled at his youthful appearance, at the same time scoffing at the Lord who had chosen David to save his people.

But the boy whom God directed, with a steady hand and by a simple throw, inflicted on the colossus a deadly wound, and thus the Lord was pleased to deliver Israel.

In the same manner as David, Thou, oh, Lord, callest us to great battles. To succeed in them in a way creditable to Thee, make us faithful as David, and then every one would perceive that the Lord is with us as He was with Israel.

And if evil sorrounds us, and if it become stronger than ourselves, then, kneeling, we shall implore Thee, Who rejectest none, and then in answer to our prayers, Thou shalt fight for us.

A. de Chambrier.

XXI.

THE TWIN SPIRITS.

TO MISS NORA HILLARY, TEACHER OF MUSIC.

I.

The sun was near the end of his journey,—the air was filled with mystery,—the violets send their odor to God,—the murmur of the stream was more lively,—all creation seemed to repeat the words of love, and my heart was seized by a pious feeling which sweetly suggested prayer.

Prostrating myself before the rustic altar of the queen of heaven, a divine pity moved my soul and I wept and prayed.

II.

Whilst to the throne of the Almighty, like a cloud of incense, joined to the sublime austere voice of the organ rose the prayer of the worshippers so dear to Him, suddenly I heard a sweet, strong, harmonious voice which troubled my heart and forced me to weep.

Raising my eyes there appeared before me a young orator, beautiful and divine in appearance who struck my heart.

III.

For many and many days already the fair young man had turned and returned around my house, looked at me and smiled, and every day I saw his sweet image; blushing, I too had answered his salute,—and each time he came I lost my peace.

God grant that he may understand me as I understand him! And if he understands me and will give me his heart I will adore him with an intense love.

IV.

He **loves, yes,** he loves me! Oh, **celestial delight!**—Ineffable **joy!**—Supreme gladness! No, **this, is not** a dream, he has told **me** and his words are words **of divine** consent. Yes, my be**loved, I will** love thee,—to thee I will open the most hidden recesses of my heart,—entirely thine will **be** this my living soul. Sweetly, sweetly a breath of **love** slighty touches my face. He **has looked** at me and placed on **my finger** a ring,—a glittering **circle of** gold.

V.

See, see how the torches shine! How beautiful **is the** altar festally adorned! How many garlands! How **much incense,** and how many lights! Oh, what a solemn funct**ion is this** one! How bright a **day,** and how the heaven smiles! I will adorn **my** head with **the** nuptial crown. **I will** appear beautiful under **my veil.** Already the harmonious trumpet **tunes** joyful songs. Oh, **my** faithful one! dost **thou** not hear the people's **shouts.**—" Hurrah! for the bride! "

VI.

" Thou **art** married. " So said the priest,—the old man, thou knowest, who **loves** me so much! **Art thou then mine?** Wilt thou be **always** at my **side?** Is then accomplished **the** hope **of my** heart? But tell me, dear, why so sadly lookest thou at **the** ground, and sighest? What thought comes **to** abate **the** course of our joy? Thinkest thou perhaps **of** thy mother whom **thou** hast left alone? **We will** go to her, but do not weep any more.

VII.

Three days **are** passed, and he **has** not returned! Already three days, **three eternal days!** and I am dying! My treasure has told me nothing. At dawn he kissed me, and quickly went away. Has he been to console his mother? But then he ought to return without delay! Pray, bright stars, bring him back to me. Without my beloved I am failing, and I will preserve alive for him the only pride of my life, with whom I fell in so great a love.

VIII.

Alas! What are these melancholy voices,—this sad sound of bells,—this grief which invades all the passers by? What wants this yet distant crowd? Somebody is dead....and is accompanied to his home by weeping faces! Alas! is it true this my horrid vision? No, it cannot be! Eternal God, Thou art not an unjust punisher! My mind is raving, and my thoughts are food for my sorrows.

IX.

Yes, my love is dead! The colored cheeks are now pale and the heart is silent. The refulgent pupil which before used to shine with divine ardor is now closed. God, why hast now taken him, when scarcely thou hadst granted me his sublime love? Like a little flower, which in the winter appears waving, and soon after is leafless and dies, thou, my sweet-heart, hast passed away.

X.

I am wretched, sad and alone, because they have taken away my treasure, burying him under the green sod not far from thy altar, Virgin Mary. They have laid on the coffin a few flowers, singing pious songs. Prepare for me in the same place the nuptial bed. I come to thee, my beloved, only comfort of my heart. United we shall spread our wings on the celestial shore, the everlasting love.

At the last tolling of the sad bell, well known to the

village people, when the night has come, and the honest prayer of the peasant singing to the Virgin, ascends to the spheres, when in the heaven raises the placid moon, when the breezes become milder, and all around the universe is silent, adoring the Creator, when, on the branches the feathered birds tranquilly hide their harmonious throaths in their winged arms, and in the sky the most distant worlds reappear, amidst the light vapors of the churchyard, a flame towers alone and trembling for a while, finally rests and waits.

Not long after, a sad and harmonious song is heard, and in the meanwhile one can see a like flame coming toward the first, and both mingled in one embrace, sweetly dissappear, like twins, destined to the same fate, who felt intense joy in meeting each other.

The firm belief of the people is that the apparition is the souls of the two unhappy ones who prematurely died in such great grief, and, on account of this, the believer pained for so great a misfortune, bows, and weeping, says AVE MARIA.

C. A. Morpurgo.

DOTTOR T. ROSSINI,
MEDICO-CHIRURGO.

Ufficio: 603 WASHINGTON STREET.

Ore di Ufficio: Dalle ore 8, alle 9 a. m.   Dalle ore 2 alle 4 p. m.

A. PRIANI QUILICI,
Levatrice.

LAUREATA nell'anno 1872 dalla Ra **UNIVERSITA'** di **GENOVA**.

Consultazioni sulle Malattie Uterine,
CURE SPECIALI
dell'Itterizia e Febbri Terzane

Domicilio 732, VIA VALLEJO, fra Powell e Stockton.

Ore d'Ufficio dalle 1.30, alle 3 p. m.

Farmacia Italiana

C. O. FAUDA   **Chimico e Farmacista.**

N. 1600 VIA STOCKTON, opposta alla Sala Bersaglieri.

aboratorio in preparazioni Chimiche. SPECIALTA' Italiane, Americane e Francesi. Unico preparatore dell' ELIXIR di WIGGERS per tutte le affezioni catarrali. Sciroppo di Eucaliptus Estratto composto di Salsapariglia.

PAOLO DE VECCHI,
Medico-Chirurgo,

610 MARKET STREET,   SAN FRANCISCO, CAL.

PACIFIC CONSOLIDATED PASTE CO.

V. RAVENNA & CO.,
Manufacturers of

MACCHERONI, * VERMICELLI, * FARINA, * ETC.

421-423 BATTERY ST. NEAR WASHINGTON.

www.ingramcontent.com/pod-product-compliance
Lightning Source LLC
Chambersburg PA
CBHW030244170426
43202CB00009B/626